CONTENTS

INTRODUCTION 5

CHAPTER 3

CHAPTER 4

CHAPTER 5

CHAPTER 6

INTRODUCTION

Whenever I tell people what I do for a living, they do two things. First they gasp in disbelief and say: 'You teach children games? Don't they *know* any?' Then they become misty-eyed…

'When *I* was young,' they say, with a fond smile, 'we used to play…' and a long-forgotten playground game will be lovingly recalled. *Queenie… Film Stars… I Sent A Letter to my Love… Kiss Chase…* Glorious treasures from a golden childhood, hoarded deep in memory. And though it's been 30, 40, 50 years or more since they played it, the teller remembers not only the *name* of the game but all the ritual that magically surrounded it: the rhyme; the actions; the rules; where it was played – and how *rough* it was! Then they start to remember all the other things they did in the playground: 'dipping' to choose who was on; spinning someone round to make them dizzy before a chase; marking out a den where you couldn't be tigged; playing with conkers, marbles, *knives*! All those wonderful clapping games and skipping songs… Kids just don't know them any more, do they?

And there, without realising it, they've answered their own question.

DO CHILDREN STILL PLAY?

Children do know *some* games, of course. They know games that have become standard PE fare, like *Cat and Mouse*. They know a handful of traditional games: *Stuck in the Mud; Mob; British Bulldog; Blind Man's Buff; Kingy*. They still play 'pretending' games (although computer zombies have replaced B-movie cowboys.) Conkers always make a seasonal return. Skipping is usually popular in schools where there's a skipping enthusiast on the staff (often a lunchtime supervisor), though sadly those wonderfully dextrous two-balls-against-a-wall games are unknown in recently built schools (too many glass windows; too few bricks).

So children do still play. What they lack is a repertoire – that encyclopedic knowledge of games and activities that most of us took for granted when we were young. This is understandable; times have changed. Like many youngsters, I learned my first games on the street. At the tender age of five I was left in the care of my nine-year-old brother, and we would play for hours with the other children 'from our road'. We'd run up and down the back alleys; run across the road, from kerb to kerb; swing from lamp-posts and hide behind bins. Even after dark, the games would continue under the street lamps and beyond, in the shadows.

Those were safer times. The shadows contained only the fears we took into them; the roads were quiet and traffic-free. We walked to school on our own – we weren't chaperoned to the school gates and back again. We weren't restricted to the house, with cartoons or computer games to amuse us. We had liberty. We were given the time and the space to learn games, and we did.

HOW CHILDREN USED TO PLAY

We also learned *how* to play – how to be fair, and play by the rules. *This* is the greater loss to our children. Not the canon of games – they can be taught – but that lesson *in* life *for* life was priceless. Children learning games informally – on the street, in the country, wherever – learned that cheating would not be tolerated, and a cheat would be chastised. They learned that you had to take your turn, and sometimes you wouldn't have a turn at all. This unwritten code of practice would be applied to any game subsequently brought into the playground and so although the games were often more violent, the playground was at least a fairer, more disciplined place than it is today.

The old games *were* more violent, without a doubt! In their classic book *Children's Games in Street and Playground* (Oxford Paperbacks) Iona and Peter Opie describe the game *Battering Rams*:

Two boys hold a third boy horizontally on their right shoulders with his feet forward, and try their weapon against other players mounted piggyback.

Or there's *Whackem*:

The players stand in a circle with their eyes closed and their hands behind their backs, while one of their number runs round the outside of the circle with a short piece of rope. As he runs he places the rope in somebody's hands, and the boy who receives it instantly opens his eyes and belabours his neighbour to the right of him. This neighbour, though taken by surprise, must set off around the circle as fast as he can, for he is subject to as many further blows as his pursuer can inflict upon him until he has completed the circuit and returned to the safety of his place.

THE MODERN PLAYGROUND

Clearly, these games would be wholly unacceptable in any modern playground – although if they *were* still permitted, there would be no shortage of players. Times have changed; boys have not! Interestingly, most of the traditional games that still survive in an unadulterated form are the violent ones – like *British Bulldog,* which is revered (and banned) in every school I visit. It's banned because it is highly competitive, extremely physical and therefore potentially dangerous. Of course, these are the same reasons why it is so adored! Older children love fast, furious, challenging, competitive, *physical* games. They will happily play other types of game occasionally, but given the choice the vast majority of children prefer rumbustious ones. Most boys demand them, and if they can't play them, they won't play at all. Instead they will play football, football and more football (which is… fast, furious, challenging, competitive and physical).

Football, however, brings its own problems. Most school playgrounds are simply too small to accommodate it. Players monopolise all the available space; small children are pushed over by blinkered forwards; other children retire to quiet corners, afraid of being hit by flying footballs.

'What we need,' says an exasperated voice in the staffroom one day, 'are proper playground games. Really good ones. Kids just don't know them any more. When I was young, we used to play…' And as the long dormant seeds of childhood begin to grow, the biscuit tin is passed around a second time, because suddenly, for some strange reason, everyone is feeling just a little bit naughty…

THE GAMES IN THIS BOOK

And so, for teachers (and lunchtime supervisors) everywhere, here are some *really good* playground games. Over the years, I have played hundreds of games with thousands of children. I have talked to them about their likes and dislikes; watched them at play and noted the things they do; absorbed their culture and fashioned new games from it. I have taught games to teachers; heard their concern about the state of their playgrounds; encouraged them to teach children *how* to play. I have worked with lunchtime supervisors; harvested their knowledge; heard their frustration; raised their self-esteem. I have researched into the games people used to play; considered and tested games suggested in both old and new books; listened to anyone who has had a game to share.

This book is the result. *Primary Playground Games* is a working manual for anyone who plays games with primary-age children. It's a personal blend of games, tips and suggestions that I have polished over the years like pebbles in a pocket. The games are a mixture of traditional and modern; some of them are completely new, devised by myself with the help of children, teachers and play workers. All of them have been vigorously road tested; they work and they are safe *as long as they are played in a responsible manner.* I add this qualifier simply because no playground game can ever be guaranteed 100 per cent safe. Children fall over; they bump their heads; they cut their knees, even when they are playing 'nicely'. Beyond this, there are some children who will always spice up the safest of games into a violent variant. (There will be a name in your head even as you read this!)

GAMES ARE GOOD FOR YOU

Introducing these games to your playground will bring enormous benefits. Children are often bored at playtime, and boredom breeds bullies. Games occupy both mind and body, and they provide a welcome release of tension after lessons. Just fifteen minutes of running and chasing, shouting and screaming, will return children to their classrooms refreshed and re-energised. There are physical benefits too, of course. The British Heart Association works extensively in schools, encouraging children to skip their way to a healthier heart.

Games are also good for promoting co-operation between children, and for nurturing the caring/sharing ethos every school

desires. They highlight the need for rules and accepting responsibility for one's actions. Individual children can be helped by the support games give in developing and maintaining friendships. There might be someone in the class whom they find a bit daunting, but if they play a game with them – well, it's easier than holding a conversation, and suddenly they don't seem quite so intimidating! Children who know plenty of games are always popular, and children who join in are perceived as happy-go-lucky, good-fun types. Finally, to return to bullying, children who play games protect themselves from bullies, who (being essentially cowardly) prefer solitary victims. They are unlikely to challenge a gang of noisy, carefree players.

GAMES FOR EVERYONE

Primary Playground Games contains something for everyone. There are games to appeal to all ages from four to eleven (and beyond! Dads will play *Twister* and *Quicksand* on a beach until they drop with exhaustion). There are different types of games: chasing games, guessing games, sitting-down games, action games and circle games. They don't need any equipment, other than an occasional piece of chalk and a blanket for two or three of them. The main requirements are imagination and a few willing friends.

The games, whatever their source, whatever their vintage, have been repackaged to excite and satisfy children of the age specified. They are perfect games for the modern playground, designed to promote positive play: games in which no one is intentionally hurt, either physically or verbally; games that are creative and encourage co-operation; games that uphold rather than challenge the school ethos. Some of the games are especially useful in this respect, and

INTRODUCTION

I have explained why in the notes given in boxes. Some of the games you might know; I make no apologies for them! They are the classics, passed on from one scabby-kneed generation to the next and included here because it would be a mistake to assume that *everyone* knows them. They don't. Through neglect and undervalue, even the best-known games are disappearing faster than peat bogs, and if inclusion here can slow their decline, I will be satisfied.

GAMES THAT WILL LAST

Most importantly, they are games that will endure. Children will enjoy them, and play them over and over again. If they are changed in the process – renamed, reinvented, re-ruled – that's fine by me! I really don't mind. All I want is for them to be played, in school and out of it, for then they flourish and survive. Recently I had the greatest compliment paid to me by children who were blissfully unaware of the fact. I was working with a class of seven-year-olds when I announced: 'The next game is called *Dead Man Arise!*'

'Oh Miss,' they groaned. 'We know that one.'

And I smiled, because I had visited that school four years previously and *no one* had known it then…

Note: there are many regional variations for the word to describe either the 'magic touch' that children use, or the chasing game itself – 'tig', 'tag', 'tick' or 'touch', just to name a few! I have chosen to use 'tig' throughout, simply because it is the term I encounter most often. Equally, there are variations for the chaser; 'on' or 'it' or a combination of the two ('on it') are all popular, but I have chosen 'on'.

GAMES FOR INFANTS

Here's a question for you. What do you call something that requires the ability to co-operate with others, an acceptance of boundaries, an understanding of rules, the willingness to relinquish power, a sense of common purpose and, perhaps, some skill at role-playing? The answer, of course, is a playground game: an extraordinarily sophisticated social activity that anyone over the age of six would casually describe as 'easy'. And games *are* easy… once you know *how* to play, and that knowledge is something that only comes with time. The magical age is around five. Under-fives *play*, of course: on their own as babies, then one-to-one with an adult; side by side with another toddler, and finally *with* the other toddler. But to play *games*, children have to develop beyond this into *co-operative play* (as the educational psychologists call it). Only then will a child be capable of taking turns, understanding and obeying rules, and playing games without an adult leader.

There is a simple way of assessing infants' ability to play games. Gather a group together and teach them how to play a chasing game like *Stuck in the Mud* (see page 16), then choose a chaser and begin. If the children have all reached the required stage, they will play the game beautifully. If they haven't, they will run off like a herd of stampeding buffalo, cheerfully unaware that the game is happening somewhere *behind* them! In a hall, they will run round and round in a circle, all in the same direction, totally self-absorbed, unsure why they're running but enjoying it anyway. Chances are, the chaser won't be tigging anyone; somebody will be tigging everyone he passes; those who *are* tigged won't stop running; some will stand still with their arms out even though they haven't been tigged… It's chaos! Joyous, spontaneous, carefree chaos. It's fun; they're playing – but they still have a little more growing to do before they can enjoy 'true' games. In the meantime, they will be quite happy playing nursery games.

Nursery games are among the most loved and best remembered of all games. Sometimes they're not really games at all; they are based on shared enjoyment rather than competition. They are safe and familiar; they feature rhymes and songs that are comfortingly repetitive; they are very simple, and easy to learn. But the best thing of all, from a child's point of view, is that they are led by a grown-up.

Children can play nursery games from the age of three, when they develop the ability to 'follow the leader', and many favourite nursery games utilise this skill. Just think of *Simon Says* or the game *Follow the Leader* itself. The children don't need to think; they just have to copy, and the model is usually a teacher or a lunchtime supervisor. In singing games like *Ring-a-Ring o' Roses*, the adult is

Older infants might also enjoy some of the easier games in the juniors section, like *King of the Wind* (see page 26) and *Jack Frost and the Sun* (also page 26).

there to lead the dance and remember all the words. Children find this very reassuring, and also delight in the fact that the adult has taken time out from her big grown-up world to play a game with them.

As long as there is a clear demonstration to begin with, children themselves can play the leading role in games such as *What's the Time, Mr Wolf?* and suddenly *they* can feel the giddy excitement of being in control of a game; of having everyone following *them*; of being the centre of attention. The taste of power is potent, and all the sweeter for being new.

In this chapter, I have arranged the games to follow an infant's development. I begin with nursery games, and these all have a strong focus, something that little ones can hold onto and follow, whether it's an action, a rhyme, a visual idea or a character. The later games begin to explore the elements of play: being on; taking turns; sharing and caring; playing safely; winning and losing.

TEACHER'S TIP

Teaching how to tig

Left to their own devices, children do not tig gently. They thump, push, slap, grab and pull each other's clothes! If you want to curb this behaviour, it is important to teach children how to tig properly, and they need to learn early, before bad habits take hold. The best time to do this is when they naturally start playing games; this shows they are beginning to explore the concept.

To begin, explain what a tig is. I usually describe it as a 'magic touch'. It's magic because when someone is tigged, something magic happens. Give some examples from games they know:

In *Stuck in the Mud*, if you are tigged, suddenly you are stuck! You can't move! It's like someone has cast a spell on you. It's magic. And in *Wake up, Sleepy Head!*, if Sleepy Head tigs

you, then **you** are the new Sleepy Head!
Something always happens when you are tigged. That's why it's magic.

Now the children know what you are talking about, you can expand on the idea that it just needs to be a touch – not a slap or a punch. I usually ask children to tig their own leg, again and again and again. Then I stop them and tell them that if their leg is feeling sore, they were tigging too hard! If they tig their friends that hard, it will hurt them, and they don't want to do *that*, do they? Then they try again, tigging more gently and saying 'Tig!' as they do so because (as I explain) in the excitement of a game, sometimes people don't feel a tig (especially if they are wearing a coat). If they call out 'Tig!' at the same time, their friends will *know* they have been caught and so they won't argue about it.

UP THE LADDERS

(FOR 3 OR MORE PLAYERS, AGE 4+)

You will need: coloured chalks

Show the children how to draw a ladder on the playground, then encourage them to draw ladders of their own. The ladders should be wide enough and long enough for the children to walk up.

Everyone holds hands in a chain. An adult leads the chain around the playground at walking pace, visiting each ladder in turn. At every ladder, the leader says this rhyme as she leads the chain up the ladder:

One – two – three
Follow me
Up the ladder
Carefully!

UP THE LADDERS

ROUND AND ROUNDY!

(FOR 4 OR MORE PLAYERS, AGE 4+)

Everyone holds hands in a circle and says this rhyme:

Here we go up and up!
(Everyone raises their hands in the air like arches.)
Here we go down and downy!
(Everyone brings their hands down.)
Here we go in!
(Still holding hands, everyone takes a small jump into the circle.)
Here we go out!
(Everyone jumps back out.)
Here we go round and roundy!
(Everyone skips to the left.)

The rhyme begins again.

> Make up a simple tune to accompany the words.

BEES IN THE HIVE

(FOR 4 OR MORE PLAYERS, AGE 4+)

The children huddle together, with heads down, and say this rhyme:

Here is the beehive
But where are the bees?
Hidden away where nobody sees.

Soon they come creeping
Out of the hive.
One – two
Three – four – five!

Buzz! Buzz! Buzz!
And back in the hive!

On 'Soon they come creeping' the children start to unfurl, and on 'Buzz! Buzz! Buzz!' they pretend to beat tiny little wings! They buzz around on the spot, and buzz greetings to their friends. On 'And back in the hive', the children huddle together again and the rhyme is repeated.

> This is good played as a parachute game, with four or five children moving about beneath a held parachute.

BEES IN THE HIVE

BIG TREE

(FOR 10 OR MORE PLAYERS, AGE 5+)

The children form a standing circle and hold hands. William is in the middle. He is the Big Tree. William mimes growing from a seed (in a crouching position) into a tree with spreading branches, while the children walk clockwise round him, singing this song:

The trees grow tall,
(The children raise their hands high into the air.)
But the leaves must fall.
(The children lower their hands.)
When the wind blows,
When the wind blows.

The children stop circling and start blowing at the tree. William mimes the tree swaying in the wind. Then he shakes himself vigorously and the other children must fly like leaves, because William is about to start chasing them!

William catches Daniel; Daniel becomes the next Big Tree.

- This is a particularly good game for autumn term.
- Make up a simple tune to accompany the words.

BIG TREE

SUNDAY RUNAWAY

(FOR 8 OR MORE PLAYERS, AGE 5+)

Everyone stands in a circle and holds hands. Carmel is on; she stands in the middle. In unison, the children chant as they creep towards her, taking one step forward for each word:

SUNDAY RUNAWAY

Monday!
Tuesday!
Wednesday!
Thursday!
Friday!
Saturday!
Sunday!
Runaway!

On 'Runaway!', they break hands and run away while Carmel chases them. She catches Joel; he is on in her place and the game begins again.

HEDGEHOGS
(FOR 12 OR MORE PLAYERS, AGE 5+)

You will need: an old blanket
Kieran is on. Everyone else snuffles around on the ground, pretending to be a hedgehog. Suddenly Kieran claps his hands, and all the hedgehogs curl up into tight balls, with their eyes closed.

HEDGEHOGS

Kieran covers one of the hedgehogs completely with the blanket. He claps his hands again, and all the hedgehogs uncurl. Then they gather round the hidden child, and try to guess who is missing.

CLASS:	**It's Darren!**
TEACHER:	**Is it Darren?**

(No response.)

CLASS:	**It's Billie!**
TEACHER:	**Is it Billie?**

(No response.)

CLASS:	**It's Alice!**
TEACHER:	**Is it Alice?**

Alice throws off the blanket and the teacher leads the children in applause to welcome Alice back. Alice is now on, and the game begins again.

> • *Always* take note of who the concealed child is, just in case you have to give clues!
>
> • Note that the previously hidden hedgehog is on in the following round – *not* the person who guesses correctly. This removes any possible benefit to peeping, and therefore helps reduce cheating.

LITTLE BABY
(FOR 6 OR MORE PLAYERS, AGE 5+)

The children stand in a line facing the leader ('Mum') who stands a fair way away and says:

> **Little Baby – Suck your thumb!**
> *(The children suck their thumbs.)*
> **Little Baby – Come to Mum!**
> *(The children teeter like babies towards the leader.)*
> **Little Baby – Smelly pants!**
> *(The children stand still, hold their noses and fan the air behind their bottoms!)*
> **Little Baby – Dance! Dance! Dance!**
> *(The children dance on the spot.)*

The rhyme is repeated until the children reach the leader, who chases them back to the starting point on a 'Come to Mum!' line and the game begins again.

> With children who can say the rhyme on their own, the leader tigs someone on the way back, and that child becomes the new leader.

DUCK DUCK GOOSE
(FOR 10 OR MORE PLAYERS, AGE 5+)

The children sit in a circle on the floor. Leon is on; he walks around the outside of the circle in a clockwise direction, tapping everyone gently on the head in turn, saying 'Duck… Duck… Duck…' Finally he taps Geeta and cries 'Goose!' and then the chase begins! Geeta leaps to her feet and pursues Leon, who runs clockwise around the circle as fast as he can. Leon tries to claim Geeta's empty place before she catches him. If he succeeds, Geeta is on in Leon's place. If he is caught, Geeta rejoins the circle and Leon must stay on for another round.

> With very young children, I usually teach them this game using a handkerchief first. The chaser silently walks around the circle holding a handkerchief, which is dropped into someone's lap to begin the chase. Once the children can play this, I substitute the words for the handkerchief.

ONE BROWN MOUSE

WAKE UP, SLEEPY HEAD!

(FOR 10 OR MORE PLAYERS, AGE 5+)

You will need: an old blanket

The children form a standing circle and hold hands. Toby is on. He is Sleepy Head and he lies on the ground and covers himself with a blanket. The children walk clockwise around him, chanting:

> **Wake up, Sleepy Head!**
> **Wake up, Sleepy Head!**

When Toby decides the time is right (usually after four to five wake-up calls), he throws off the blanket, leaps up and chases the other children. He catches Emma, and she becomes the new Sleepy Head.

> *Dead Man Arise!* (see page 25) is the junior version of this game.

ONE BROWN MOUSE

(FOR SMALL GROUPS OF 6 OR 7 PLAYERS, AGE 5+)

The children stand in a row and lean with both their hands against a wall, forming a tunnel. They say:

> **One brown mouse,**
> **Very, very small,**
> **Ran through a hole in the kitchen wall.**

On 'Ran through a hole', the child at the top of the line runs through the tunnel and rejoins the line at the far end. The rhyme continues until all the children have run through.

- This can be used as a counting game, with '*Two* brown mice' and '*Three* brown mice' and so on.
- Note that only one child runs at a time, even if the rhyme says two or three.

STUCK IN THE MUD

(FOR 12 OR MORE PLAYERS, AGE 5+)

Hannah is on. She chases the others and tigs Rosie. Now Rosie is stuck in the mud! She must stand still, with her arms and legs outstretched, and wait for someone to help her.

Jayne runs up to Rosie, runs beneath one of her arms and the spell is broken. Rosie is free to run again. The game is over when everyone is stuck in the mud.

- There are many variations of this game. Sometimes players are released by the rescuer running between their legs. This variant is still generally known as *Stuck in the Mud*, but in some regions it is called *Underground Tig*. Sometimes the runners stand with just their arms outstretched (not their legs). This variant is called *Scarecrow Tig*.
- Players can be tigged while attempting a rescue.
- Since the chaser is on throughout the game, you might need more than one, depending on the number of players.

RAINBOWS

(FOR 15 OR MORE PLAYERS, AGE 5+)

Caron is on. Everybody else forms a pair and holds their partner's hand. Caron chases the pairs, and when she tigs a pair – either partner, not both – that pair must stop running, fully join hands and raise them into the air, forming an arch or rainbow. The pair must remain in that position until they are released by another pair running under the rainbow.

The game is over when all the pairs are rainbows.

- Rescuers can be tigged while attempting a rescue.
- The game is equally popular with older children when renamed *Arch Tig*.

MOTHER HUBBARD

(FOR 6 OR MORE PLAYERS, AGE 5+)

Familiarise the children with the nursery rhyme 'Old Mother Hubbard', if they do not know it:

Old Mother Hubbard
Went to the cupboard
To get her poor dog a bone,
But when she got there
The cupboard was bare
And so the poor dog had none.

Flora is on. She is Mother Hubbard and she stands with her back to the others, who form a line facing her some distance away. The others creep forward, while they chant:

What's in your cupboard, Mother Hubbard?

Then they *stand still* while Flora turns to face them. She names something in her cupboard – cheese, butter, biscuits and so on – and then turns away again.

The other children creep forward again, repeating the question; again Flora turns and answers them. Finally (when the others are getting really close), Flora answers: 'Bones!' and the others run away screaming, back to the starting line. But Flora is in hot pursuit! She catches Kim, and Kim becomes the next Mother Hubbard.

HUGGY BEAR TIG

(FOR 10 OR MORE PLAYERS, AGE 5+)

A fast, funny 'feel good' game

Kelly is on. Everyone else runs away and she chases them, but she cannot tig them if they are hugging somebody! As soon as Kelly runs by, the huggers must break up and run again.

Kelly manages to tig Ruth. Ruth is now on, and Kelly is free to run with the others.

- Players can hug in twos, in threes or in groups.
- If the children are still new to tigging, the game is easier for them to follow if the chaser carries a brightly coloured rag which is passed on to the next chaser.

CHICKEN RUN

(FOR 10 OR MORE PLAYERS, AGE 6+)

Two children form an arch: the entrance to a chicken shed; they are also the lookout. The other children huddle close together behind the arch, in the shed. At this stage, the shed has invisible walls; the chickens are safe but…

CHICKEN RUN

Outside the shed, John is on. He is the fox, and he circles it, frightening the chickens by sniffing them and drooling: 'Chickens… I smell chickens!' When John feels the time is right, he dashes through the entrance arch and the two lookouts cry: 'Cock-a-doodle-do!' The chickens scatter; the walls have disappeared. John catches three people: the first is the new fox, and the next two form a new arch. The game begins again.

• *Chicken Run* really does need demonstrating well, so an adult should be the first fox. With *very* small children, an adult can play the fox throughout, with the chase simply determining who will be the next arch.

• Sometimes children will bring down their arms like a guillotine to stop the fox as he tries to enter. (They are remembering *Oranges and Lemons*, I think, with 'Here comes a chopper to chop off your head.') This is not their job at all! The fox is supposed to have free access, whenever he chooses. The lookouts' role is simply to raise the alarm, and this must be made clear before the game begins.

THE FLY AND THE BUMBLE BEE

(FOR 12 OR MORE PLAYERS, AGE 6+)

The children form two equal lines and face each other. In one line, they are bees. In the other, they are flies. Together, they chant this rhyme:

> **Fiddle de dee! Fiddle de dee!**
> **The fly has married the bumble bee**
> **In a church for all to see,**
> **The fly has married the bumble bee!**

For the first two lines, the children simply clap four beats. On 'In a church for all to see', the children hold hands with the child directly opposite them, forming a wedding arch. On the final 'The fly has married…', the two children at the top of the line join hands and skip down under the arch. They rejoin the line at the end and the rhyme begins again.

STICKY WITCH

(FOR 15 OR MORE PLAYERS, AGE 6+)

You will need: chalk

Chalk three circles on the ground, big enough to hold everyone playing the game. These are glue pots, and they are guarded by the Sticky Witch.

Sara is the Sticky Witch. Everyone runs around and between her glue pots, while she chases them. When she catches someone, she puts them into a glue pot, where they become sticky too! The captives stretch out their sticky fingers like sea anemones, and any passing runner they touch must join them in the pots.

Once everyone is held captive in the pots, the witch pretends to take up a big spoon. She stirs the pots, the glue gets hotter and hotter, and the captives noisily melt away to nothing!

The last child caught becomes the next Sticky Witch and the game begins again.

• This game needs to be clearly demonstrated. Walk it through first, so the children can see exactly what they must do once they are in the pots.

• A potential problem with *Sticky Witch* is that some children will run far beyond the reach of the captives. This is simply because they know that the last person caught will be the next witch. You will need to stress the playing area before you begin to play. I warn them with 'If I see you running too far away, I'll put you in the pot myself!' This usually does the trick!

• A good game for encouraging children to tig *everyone* – not just their friends.

• *Mummy Hunt* is a junior version of this game (see page 25).

THE GINGERBREAD MAN

(FOR 10 OR MORE PLAYERS, AGE 6+)

Keith is on, and he stands in the middle of a standing circle. He asks the other children – the runners – a series of questions, and they answer him:

KEITH:	**Where have you been?**
RUNNERS:	**Down the lane.**
KEITH:	**What did you see?**
RUNNERS:	**A little white house.**
KEITH:	**Who was there?**
RUNNERS:	**The Gingerbread Man.**
KEITH:	**What did he say?**
RUNNERS:	*Catch me if you can!*

The runners flee. Keith catches Khurram; he is the new chaser and the game begins again.

CHOP! CHOP!

(FOR 12 OR MORE PLAYERS, AGE 6+)

Everyone stands in a circle. Clare is on. She walks clockwise round the outside of the circle, holding one arm high in the air like a big chopper. Suddenly she stops, and brings her arm down, slicing the air between Glynn and Ayesha, saying 'Chop! Chop!' as she does so.

Glynn and Ayesha run around the circle, in opposite directions, while Clare stands in the place they have vacated, facing inwards and a little back from the circle, holding out her hands with palms upturned. Glynn runs faster round the circle. He tigs Clare first, so he is the new chopper. Ayesha simply rejoins the circle, and the game begins again.

- With two fast runners it can look like a dead heat, so it is important they tig the outstretched hands. Equally, the other players should be made to realise that only the chopper truly knows who was the faster runner, because their fingers gave him that crucial information. It doesn't matter what it *looked* like; it's what it *felt* like that is important.

- *Blade* is a junior version of this game (see page 28).

FIVE CURRANT BUNS

(FOR 10 OR MORE PLAYERS, AGE 6+)

Five children are chosen to be the currant buns. They stand in a line facing the others, who huddle together and decide who they are going to 'buy' first.

The 'buyers' chant this rhyme, creeping closer to the buns as they do so:

> **Five currant buns in a baker's shop,**
> **Big and round with a cherry on the top.**
> **Along we came with a penny one day,**
> **Bought a currant bun and *took it away*!**

On 'took it away', the buyers seize the bun they have chosen, and take him back to their side. Then they huddle together again and decide who to buy next. The chant becomes '*Four* currant buns in a baker's shop' and the game continues.

FIVE CURRANT BUNS

TUNNEL TIG

TUNNEL TIG
(FOR 12 OR MORE PLAYERS, AGE 7+)

Aaron is on, and he chases the other children. He tigs Bethany; she must run to the nearest wall and lean with one hand against it, waiting to be rescued. Aaron tigs Joshua, then Robyn; they too must lean against the wall, and they stand next to Bethany, forming a little tunnel.

Connor decides to rescue his friends. He runs beneath the tunnel of arms, and the three captives are free to run again.

- Captives can be rescued singly or in groups.
- The captives don't have to make one big tunnel. With a whole class playing, it's common to see half a dozen tunnels, spread along two or more walls.

THE GOLDEN POT
(FOR 8 OR MORE PLAYERS, AGE 6+)

You will need: chalk, preferably yellow
Using the chalk, the children draw a pitch like this:

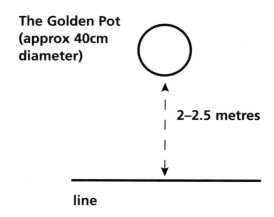

The Golden Pot (approx 40cm diameter)

2–2.5 metres

line

Explain to the children that the fairies are very, very old creatures and extremely wise. They are full of magic, and they don't want Big People like ourselves to know their secrets.

The Golden Pot is a special magic place where they hide their secrets. A fairy guards it all the time, but if a Big Person puts their hand inside that pot, some of the fairy magic instantly passes into him, making him into a wiser person. So the aim of the game is for the Big People to touch the pot while the fairy isn't looking.

Shannon is on. She is the fairy. The other children stand behind the line, but one at a time, as often as they can, they dash to the Golden Pot and touch it. But Shannon is on guard, and she tigs Jodie. Jodie is now the new fairy, and the game continues.

- This game can be played 'in the round' with the Golden Pot placed inside a chalk circle. I usually call this version *Fairy Ring*.
- *Zombie Pit* is a junior version of *Fairy Ring* (see page 30).

THE GOLDEN POT

FISHES IN THE NET
(FOR 12 OR MORE PLAYERS, AGE 6+)

Three or four of the children hold hands and form a net. Together, they pick a number between one and ten, without telling the other children what this number is. Then they hold their hands up in the air and start counting aloud: 'One – two – three – four' while the other children (the fish) walk in and out, underneath their arms. When the net children reach the number they chose, they bring their hands down. Any fish caught in the net must become part of the net. A new number is chosen and the game continues until all the fish have been caught.

FISHES IN THE NET

JELLY ON A PLATE
(FOR 7 OR MORE PLAYERS, AGE 7+)

Candice is on. She stands with her back to the other players, who make a line facing her some distance away. Candice asks the others a series of questions, always beginning with:

Do you like...?

She might ask about food ('Do you like chips? Do

you like toast?'). She might ask about hobbies ('Do you like swimming?'). Or pop stars, or television programmes – whatever she fancies!

The other players must answer her, but only if their answer is yes. They must be *truthful*. So if their answer is yes, they shout 'Yes!' and take one step forward. If their answer is no, they stay silent and stand still. For example:

CANDICE:	**Do you like baked beans?**
POLLY/JOANNE/URSULA:	**Yes!**

(All three girls take one step forward.)

CANDICE:	**Do you like chocolate?**
POLLY/JOANNE/URSULA:	**Yes!**

(They take another step forward.)

CANDICE:	**Do you like peas?**
POLLY/JOANNE:	**Yes!**

(These two take another step forward. Ursula remains silent and stays where she is.)

With every question, the players creep closer and closer to Candice. When someone gets close enough, Candice is touched on the back. She spins around and chases everyone back to the starting line. She catches Kevin; he is the new questioner and the game begins again.

But Candice doesn't have to wait to be touched. At any time during the game, she can start the chase by asking: 'Do you like *jelly on a plate*?' The players must flee back to the line, because Candice will be fast on their heels!

This is a good game for exploring truth and fairness. You can play the eagle-eyed referee! Draw attention to the size of the strides some children will be making. Some children will answer yes to everything. Are they being truthful? Encourage the questioner to ask questions which clearly should be answered no, such as 'Do you like eating worms?' It's fun to include some questions with a clear male/female bias too: 'Do you like Barbie?' Anyone who isn't playing fair can be sent back to the starting line.

CHAPTER 2

GAMES FOR JUNIORS

By the time children reach the junior playground, there is nothing they cannot do. They can choose who should be on; they can organise teams or sides; they can understand the importance of rules; they can run without falling over their own feet! Best of all, they have the imagination to refashion familiar games, or to create new ones, drawing upon contemporary culture to pep up their play. Unfortunately, some of the ways in which children do this can be worrying. Games can be extremely violent – not necessarily in a physical sense, but in a gory sense, with killings, mutilations and imaginary tortures. Like countless generations before them, today's children pretend to be their favourite film and television heroes. Clean-cut cowboys, Indians, Martians and robots have been replaced by computer zombies, mummies and vampires, all accompanied by the appropriate slayer, who will invariably spill buckets of imaginary blood and guts before the game is through. Is this cause for concern? I think not. It is generally accepted that one of the functions of play is that it allows children to explore the realities of our frightening adult world in a safe way. It's safe, because they are ultimately in control. Children are aware of the darker side of life: murder, abduction, war, domestic violence, death, and the supernatural. Games and play-acting allow them to explore some of these issues in broad daylight and in the comforting company of friends. Children are curious; they will experiment, one way or another, and to flirt with the fear of death playing *Dead Man Arise!* (see page 25) is surely safer than sneaking off to a graveyard at midnight. Of course, if you oppose the games on religious grounds, that is entirely a different matter. Equally, if war games become 'personal' between ethnic groups, action must be taken, and in many cases, games can be used constructively as a way of opening the debate on social issues.

In some schools, the content of the games isn't the concern: it's their sheer *physicality*. So much running, chasing, catching! Many times I have been called into schools by heads who would like quiet, creative games that don't involve running. I do have such games in my repertoire but unfortunately, children *prefer* chasing games. Games should *excite*, and it's difficult to generate excitement when you're stationary! There's nothing like the thrill of a chase to make the adrenalin flow. Add to this the glory of catching someone – or the elation of getting away – and it's easy to see why chasing games are the clear favourites with most children.

In this chapter there are plenty of chasing games, but also circle, action and guessing games. The chasing games have been designed for playgrounds with limited space. Many contain a focus: something that will gather the players back together at regular intervals so the

Young juniors might also enjoy these games from 'Games for infants': Sunday Runaway (see page 14), Hedgehogs (see page 15), Little Baby (see page 15), Chicken Run (see page 17), Sticky Witch (see page 18), Tunnel Tig (see page 20), Fishes in the Net (see page 21) and Jelly on a Plate (see page 21).

game doesn't become 'free-roaming' over the entire play area. Often this focus is a 'suspense' or a 'delayed' start – a device that helps slower runners enormously (see page 57 for a full explanation). Circle games like *Blade* (see page 28) are popular with runners who tire easily, because they know they will only have to run around the circle. Action games like *Charlie's Angels* (see page 36) have a physical content but no chase at all. Guessing games like *Pop Stars* (see page 32) are usually favourites with girls, who like a tiny bit of competitive running and a generous helping of intrigue. There's only one holding-hands-in-a-circle game, because children over the age of eight squirm at the thought of such contact, but *Dead Man Arise!* is such fun that even eleven-year-old boys will suffer the indignity of holding hands for the sake of its excellent chase.

Several of the games involve drawing pitches with chalk. All children adore chalk, and the pleasure in these games is often derived more from the pitch marking than from the game itself! You will have to draw a demonstration pitch first, but then you should give the children chalk to draw their own. *Never make them play on a pitch you have drawn!* Some teachers see children 'struggling' with wonky lines and misshapen squares, step in to make sure the pitch is 'right' and steal the fun in the process. Please leave them to it!

Other games include *Wizards, Giants and Dwarves* (see page 30) for young strategists everywhere, and the physically demanding *Quicksand* (see page 37), which can tame the wildest of boys.

Like the previous selection in Chapter 1, the games are listed in an order that ascends with age. Unlike games for younger children, however, it's not just a question of difficulty: it's also a question of *appeal*. Perhaps it would be truer to say that they are listed in order of increasing *sophistication*. A game like *Spider* (see page 35), for example, seems very simple, but there's a psychological edge to it that is quite beyond the grasp of seven-year-olds. Some of the later games are really quite complex: litanies of rules and instructions, requiring both comprehension and adherence. They are truly challenging, as they *must* be, to command the respect of ten- to eleven-year-olds. Not that anyone will ever *admit* they are challenging. They're *easy*. Dead simple, Miss. If you're ten. If you're forty, you may wonder how anyone can ever learn them all, let alone explain them to new players, but they can. Such are the joys and mysteries of childhood!

TEACHER'S TIP

Talking about running

Running ability isn't something that children think about. They can tell you who is the fastest (and the slowest) in the class, and they all know roughly where they fit on the scale in between, but they never seem to consider the consequences of such variation. They simply accept running ability as a fact; it's not seen as a problem and so they don't seek solutions. Instead, the slowest runner in the class will find himself being the person who is on all playtime, wheezing and groaning, while his friends run past him, indifferent to his physical discomfort. No one suggests playing a different game – not even the slow runner himself! He will just struggle on, because the alternative – watching from the sidelines – is too awful to contemplate.

Whenever I teach juniors *Blade* (see page 28), I always begin with a short discussion about running. It's easy to engage them:

Who thinks they are a fast runner?
Who thinks they are a slow runner?
Who thinks they are fast – but know they tire easily?
Who thinks they are slow – but know they can keep going for ages?

Then you can explain that we are all different runners. I usually say something like this:

Some people are fast; some are slow. We can't all be fast, explosive runners. That's a gift. Just as some people are good at singing, or can paint beautifully or are brilliant swimmers, some people can run really fast. That's *their* gift. But if you're not a good runner, some games can be *awful*. Games like *Tig*, where someone shouts out, 'One – two – three!' and everyone runs to the far end of the playground. And if *you're* on, by the time you catch up with everyone else, you're worn out! It's hard work! It's just not *fun* any more.

So, if you're that kind of runner – or if you get tired easily – then it's a good idea to know some different games. Ones where you don't have to run too far or for too long. *Circle* games are good for that, because you *know* that you will only have to run around the circle. And a really good circle game is *Blade*...

After *Blade,* you can try some of the games with suspense starts, like *Spider* (see page 35) or *Poison* (see page 28), and ask the slower runners whether they found that type of start useful.

Discussing running like this helps the children to realise that some of their friends might find running games difficult, but *there are alternatives*, and in the name of fairness and equality, they should be explored. And because the games are good ones, slower runners can feel confident in suggesting them at playtime too.

DEAD MAN ARISE!

(FOR 8 OR MORE PLAYERS, AGE 7+)

You will need: an old blanket

The children form a standing circle and hold hands. Ian is on. He is the Dead Man and he lies on the ground and covers himself with a blanket. The children walk clockwise around him, chanting:

Dead Man Arise!
Dead Man Arise!

When Ian decides the time is right (usually after four to five repeats of the line), he throws off the blanket, leaps up and chases the other children. He catches Tripta, and she becomes the new Dead Man.

- This is a Victorian game, and the chant has always been 'Dead Man Arise!', but in these PC times some of the children may say it should be Dead Girl or whatever. It's up to you how you deal with this, but it's worth remembering that the benefit of a rhyme lies in the fact that it *does* stay the same! It's comforting to know the words, and to know they're not going to change. If they *do* change, some children might not join in because they are worried about getting them wrong. I also like the idea of keeping the traditional game alive with its original words intact, but having said that, this game is equally popular with infants, using the less scary *Wake up, Sleepy Head!* (see page 16).

- If you want to introduce your children to the Big Red Tomato card discipline aid (see 'How to transform your playground' page 54), this is the perfect game to use! Being on is *so* popular in this game that 'tomatoes' appear everywhere. Explain how the card works and why you're using it, then play the game and start flashing!

MUMMY HUNT

(FOR 12 OR MORE PLAYERS, AGE 7+)

You will need: chalk

Chalk three circles on the ground, large enough to hold everyone playing the game. These are the mummy pits.

Farrah is on; she is the archaeologist. The other players (the mummies) run around and between the mummy pits, while she chases them. When Farrah catches someone, she puts them into a pit, and although they cannot come out of the pit, they *can* stretch out their arms like sea anemones, and any passing runner they touch must join them in the pits.

Once everyone is held captive in the pits, Farrah pretends to pull a lever beside each pit, and the mummies fall down into oblivion!

The last person caught becomes the next archaeologist and the game begins again.

- This game needs to be clearly demonstrated. Walk it through first, so children can see exactly what they must do once they are in the pits.

- A potential problem with *Mummy Hunt* is that some children will run far beyond the reach of the captives. This is simply because they know that the last person caught will be the next archaeologist. You will need to stress the playing area before you begin to play. I warn them with 'If I see you running too far away, I'll put you in a pit myself!' This usually does the trick!

- A good game for encouraging children to tig *everyone* – not just their friends.

- *Sticky Witch,* (see page 18), an infant version of this game, is also perfectly acceptable to juniors up to the age of nine.

DEAD MAN ARISE!

KING OF THE WIND

JACK FROST AND THE SUN

(FOR 12 OR MORE PLAYERS, AGE 7+)

Two children are on. Ryan is Jack Frost and Molly is the Sun. Ryan tigs Caitlin; she must 'freeze' and cannot move until she is 'thawed' – that is, tigged again by Molly.

> This is a good game for enlivening a PE lesson. Jack Frost can wear a blue band, while the Sun wears a yellow one.

KING OF THE WIND

(FOR 12 OR MORE PLAYERS, AGE 7+)

You will need: chalk
Draw this compass on the playground:

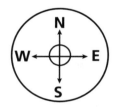

circle diameter approx 1 metre

Liam is on. He is the King of the Wind, and he stands in the middle of the compass and closes his eyes. The other players can choose where they are going to stand – North, South, East or West.

Jack chooses North. He stands about four metres away from the compass, with all those who have chosen likewise. Other children have chosen East, West or South; they too form small, loose groups. Then, in unison, all the runners chant:

North, South, East, West.
Where will the wind blow next?

and as they chant it, all four groups creep closer to the compass. *The runners must not enter the circle.* At the end of the chant, they blow three times at the King. Then the King (with his eyes still closed) calls out one of the directions – 'North!' – and all the players who had chosen to stand to the North must run away. The King opens his eyes and chases them,

while the children who had chosen East, West and South simply stand still.

Liam tigs Jack; he is the new King of the Wind and the game begins again.

> • The children may choose a new direction to stand in for each new round.
>
> • Even if you already have a compass painted on the playground, you will still need to draw the outer circle. This is a safety measure. Without it, the children will simply mob the person who is on!
>
> • Over-enthusiastic players benefit from small, chalk-starting lines (one for each compass point) approximately four metres from the circle.

SICK DOG

(FOR 8 OR MORE PLAYERS, AGE 7+)

Hazel is on; she is the Sick Dog. She tigs Husnu on his arm. Now Husnu is the Sick Dog! Hazel is healed, and can run with the others, but Husnu must hold the spot on his arm where he was tigged. Then he starts chasing.

> A lurid name for a great game! Children like games when the chaser changes within seconds, and they love tomfoolery. This is a perfect blend of both.

Husnu tigs Carl on his knee. Husnu is healed now, so he lets go of his arm and runs away with the others. Carl is the new Sick Dog, and he has to hold his knee while he chases…

> There should only be *one* Sick Dog at any one time!

TOUCH AND GO

(FOR 10 OR MORE PLAYERS, AGE 7+)

Aimee and Seren are on. They hold hands and chase the others. Seren tigs Melissa and exchanges places with her. So now Aimee and *Melissa* (holding hands) are on, while Seren is free to run with the others.

Aimee tigs Joseph. She exchanges places with *him*, so now Melissa and *Joseph* (holding hands) are on, while Aimee is free to run.

- With large groups, you may need two or three pairs to be on.
- Older children will probably only play this in single-sex groups! (For advice on holding hands, see 'Troubleshooting' on page 73.)

ARCH TIG

(FOR 15 OR MORE PLAYERS, AGE 7+)

This is played in exactly the same way as *Rainbows* (see 'Games for infants', page 17) but the rainbow imagery is omitted.

VAMPIRE SLAYER

(FOR 8 OR MORE PLAYERS, AGE 8+)

Scott is on. He is the Vampire Slayer, and he stands a good distance away from the other players, with his back to them. The others are vampires; they form a line and begin to creep towards him. But then, without warning, Scott turns around, and the light in his eyes is too much for the vampires to bear! Instantly, they cover their faces with their sleeves, but if Scott sees anyone's eyes, he sends them back to the starting line.

When the vampires get close enough to touch Scott, they tap him on the back. Scott turns and chases them back to the starting line. He tigs Paul. Paul is the new slayer and the game begins again.

This is basically the well-known infant game, *Grandmother's Footsteps*, repackaged to appeal to juniors.

CATS IN THE CORNER

(FOR 5 PLAYERS, AGE 8+)

You will need: a ready-painted square or rectangle, or one third of a netball court
Four players or 'cats' stand in the four corners of the square or rectangle. Sunita is on; she stands in the middle.

Using a system of nods, winks and calls, the cats exchange places. Any two cats can swap corners – even those diagonally across from each other. Sunita has to claim one of the corners while it is unguarded, and when she does, the 'homeless' cat has to be on in her place.

VAMPIRE SLAYER

POISON

BLADE

(FOR 12 OR MORE PLAYERS, AGE 8+)

Everyone stands in a circle. Palvi is on. She walks clockwise round the outside of the circle. Suddenly she stops, and holding her arm outstretched, she quickly brings it down like a sharp blade between Dale and Donna, with an accompanying blade-through-air 'Ssshhh' sound.

Dale and Donna run around the circle, in opposite directions, while Palvi stands in the place they have vacated, facing inwards with her arms outstretched and her palms upturned. Donna runs faster round the circle. She tigs Palvi first, and so she is the new Blade. Dale simply rejoins the circle, and the game begins again.

> • With two fast runners it can look like a dead heat, so it is important they tig the outstretched hands. Equally, the other players should be made to realise that only the Blade truly knows who was the faster runner, because their fingers gave them that crucial information. It doesn't matter what it *looked* like; it's what it *felt* like that is important.
>
> • *Chop! Chop!* (see page 19) is an infant version of this game.

POISON

(FOR 5 OR MORE PLAYERS, AGE 8+)

Danny is on. He holds out his arms, and stretches out his fingers. The other players each take hold of a finger. Danny asks:

Do you like...?

and it can be anything – pineapple, pear juice, purple – as long as it begins with the letter 'p'. He repeats this line, changing it every time, until he finally says:

Do you like *Poison*?

and then everyone runs away, with Danny in pursuit. The person he catches is the next one on and the game begins again.

However, if a player lets go of Danny's finger and it *wasn't* Poison, they have been *tricked* into being on, and they must swap places with Danny. So, it might go like this:

DANNY:	**Do you like pickles?**
	(No one moves.)
	Do you like Pepsi?
	(No one moves.)
	Do you like PEARS?!
	(Permosh lets go, thinking it was Poison.)

Now Permosh is on instead of Danny.

PERMOSH:	**Do you like peaches?**
	(No one moves.)
	Do you like pies?
	(No one moves.)
	Do you like pineapple?
	(No one moves.)
	Do you like POISON?!
	(Everyone runs.)

Permosh tigs Sally and the game begins again with Sally on.

SHADOW TIG

(FOR 8 OR MORE PLAYERS, AGE 8+)

You will need: a very sunny day!
Isaac is on. He chases the others, but instead of tigging someone's *body*, he has to stamp on their *shadow*. Isaac 'tigs' Dean; Dean is the new chaser.

> Best played with good friends in small groups, because the players have to trust each other.

TWISTER

TWISTER

(FOR 4 PLAYERS, AGE 8+)

Jonathan is on. He covers his ears while the other three players stand away from him and number themselves 1, 2 and 3. Then they join hands, forming a tight triangle.

When they're ready, Jonathan calls out a number: '2!'

'It's David!' comes the reply, and Jonathan has to tig David on his back while the other two players twist and turn to protect him. Once Jonathan succeeds, David takes his turn at being on and the game begins again.

> • A player can only be tigged on his back. You cannot lunge across the triangle to tig him on his front.
> • The three joined players must hold hands at all times.
> • For a change, try colours or pop stars instead of numbers.
> • This is a challenging game that requires considerable energy but takes up a surprisingly small amount of room, and because it encourages nifty footwork, it can also be used as a warm-up for football or netball training sessions!

TURTLE TIG

(FOR 12 OR MORE PLAYERS, AGE 8+)

Amy is on. She chases the other players and tigs Stefan; now Stefan is on. Stefan chases Harry, but Harry is going to make a turtle! He cannot be tigged if he is a turtle…

To make a turtle, Harry runs up behind Owen and puts his hands on Owen's shoulders. Owen is the turtle; Harry is the shell. Stefan cannot tig either of them.

Stefan carries on chasing. He is after Rhiannon now, but Rhiannon runs up behind Harry and puts her hands on his shoulders. She is safe! But now the turtle has two shells! This cannot be, so Owen (at the front) is jettisoned by Harry. Owen is now back in the chase.

> The turtles can walk; they don't have to stand still.

ZOMBIE PIT

(FOR 7 TO 10 PLAYERS, AGE 8+)

WIZARDS, GIANTS AND DWARVES

You will need: chalk

The children draw a pitch with the chalk (see below). Using the lines on a netball court for two sides of the square will make it much easier.

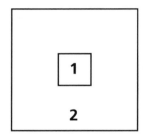

1. The Dead Zone (diameter approx 30cm)
2. The Zombie Pit (diameter approx 2–2.5m)

The Zombies have a dark place called the Dead Zone, which is the source of all their power and knowledge. They do not want anyone else to discover its secrets, so a Zombie guards it day and night. But if someone *does* manage to put his hand onto the Dead Zone square, he will gain knowledge. So the aim of the game is for the players to touch the Dead Zone while the Zombie isn't looking.

Lloyd is on. He is the Zombie, and he stands inside the Zombie Pit. The other players slip furtively in and out of the Zombie Pit, touching the Dead Zone as often as they can. But Lloyd is on guard, and he tigs Christopher. Christopher is now the new Zombie, and the game continues.

As an alternative, anyone the Zombie tigs can be turned to stone. This means the players have added obstacles between them and the Dead Zone. The last player to be caught is the new Zombie. This version is best played with a straight line, rather than a square (see *The Golden Pot* in 'Games for infants', page 20).

WIZARDS, GIANTS AND DWARVES

(FOR 2 OR MORE PLAYERS, AGE 8+)

The players divide into two teams. The two teams then huddle together and decide whether *collectively* they are going to be wizards, giants or dwarves. When both teams are ready, they stand in two lines facing each other.

Someone calls out 'One – two – three' and the teams adopt the following postures, depending on what they decided:
• Wizards: a lunge forward with an outstretched arm, like they are aiming wands
• Giants: on tiptoes with arms stretched menacingly above their heads, ferocious faces and roars
• Dwarves: crouching down, like miniature wrestlers.

The game works like *Paper–Scissors–Stone*:
Wizards beat Giants (because they can cast a spell on them)
Giants beat Dwarves (because they can stamp on them)
Dwarves beat Wizards (because they can climb up the wizards' cloaks and throttle them!).

The winning team scores a point. The first team to score ten points wins the game.

• If both teams choose the same, neither team scores.

• A fun game that requires no running whatsoever and may be tied in to Harry Potter!

• Teams do not have to contain equal numbers.

• Although the game can be played with as few as two players, it is fascinating to play it as a whole class – girls against boys.

• When played in pairs, this is a perfect indoor game for wet play.

DEVIL'S DEN

(FOR 8 OR MORE PLAYERS, AGE 8+)

Nick is on. He is the Devil. The other players must be touching him in some way (for example, touching his arm or back) while everyone chants this rhyme:

Devil's Den,
Devil's Den,
Run when you reach ten,
One – two – three – four – five – six – seven –
eight – nine – ten!

When they reach ten, all the players run away with Nick in pursuit. He tigs Dominic, and Dominic becomes a chaser too. Ben is tigged next; he too becomes a chaser.

Eventually, only Zach is still running free. Once he is tigged, Zach becomes the new Devil and the game begins again with the rhyme.

> This is an extremely energetic game, positively *adored* by strong, fast runners.

DEVIL'S DEN

HOSPITAL TIG

(FOR 6 TO 8 PLAYERS, AGE 8+)

In this chasing game, players have to be caught five times before they are out of the game. The same chaser remains on throughout.

HOSPITAL TIG

Grant is on. He tigs Della; she continues to run but holds her arm to show that she has been tigged once. Grant chases after the others.

When Della is tigged a second time, she has to hold *both* her arms. After a third tig she must 'hold' her leg – that is, run with one of her elbows touching her thigh. After a fourth tig she runs bent double, with both elbows on her thighs. After a fifth tig she must lie down on the ground 'in hospital' and await the end of the game. The last person to be hospitalised becomes the new chaser.

> • Players must be tigged on five separate occasions. A chaser cannot take all five lives at once.
>
> • Best played in summer, on a field, in small groups and away from other children, simply because prone children are at risk in a busy playground. Small groups are advised because with lots of players, it can be boring for anyone hospitalised early in the game.

TROLL TRICKER

(FOR 10 OR MORE PLAYERS, AGE 8+)

Mohammed is on. He is the Troll, and he guards an imaginary bridge. He asks the other players a question with two possible answers, for example 'What do I like on my chips: salt or vinegar?' Mohammed covers his ears while the group decides. *The whole group must agree upon the same answer.*

The group cries, 'Ready!' and Mohammed gives the answer: 'Vinegar!'

This isn't what the group chose! They have to run across the 'bridge' to the Troll's side. Mohammed catches Cheryl; she is the new Troll.

If the group guesses *correctly*, everyone can walk unmolested across the bridge. The Troll walks in the opposite direction, and once both sides are facing each other again, the Troll asks a second question.

BUZZ!

(FOR 12 OR MORE PLAYERS, AGE 8+)

You will need: chalk

On the ground, the children draw a series of small squares, each one big enough to hold just one person. Wanda is on. She runs after Theo and he flees to one of the squares. Once he is standing inside it, he is safe; Wanda cannot tig him. But Theo cannot stay there forever…

Diana is being chased. All the squares are occupied now, so she runs up to Theo and cries: 'Buzz!' Theo must vacate the square and run on. Now Diana is safe, but Theo isn't! He runs up to Harriet in another square, cries 'Buzz!' and takes over her square. Harriet runs, but she is caught by Wanda. Harriet is now on, and Wanda is free to run with the others.

> You will need to draw squares in a ratio of about 1:4 runners.

GOBLIN CHASER

(FOR 10 OR MORE PLAYERS, AGE 8+)

Meera is the Goblin. She stands apart from the others and covers her ears while they decide what colour she will be. When the others have decided, they form a circle and stand motionless, pretending to be statues. Two of the players in the circle form an arch.

Meera walks around the circle, pretending to be a goblin. 'What colour am I?' she asks. 'Am I *red*?' (No reply.) 'Am I *blue*?' (Still no reply.) 'Am I *green*?'

This is the colour the group chose! Instantly, the two players forming the arch cry out: 'Yes! Yes! Yes!' and Meera rushes underneath the arch to begin the chase. The other players flee, but Meera catches Naomi, and she becomes the new Goblin.

> This is similar to the infant game *Chicken Run* (see page 17), but the choosing of colours adds junior appeal.

POP STARS

(FOR 6 OR MORE PLAYERS, AGE 9+)

You might need: chalk

Ellie is on. She stands in between two of the shorter lines of a netball court (for example, the lines marking out the centre third). The other players stand behind one of the painted lines.

> This game is best played using the lines of a netball court, but chalk lines can be drawn instead.

Ellie thinks of a pop star and then calls out the initials of their name: 'BS!'

Maria thinks she knows the answer, so she runs across the pitch, stamps her foot beyond the far line, runs back behind the starting line and calls it out: 'Britney Spears!' If she is right, she is on instead of Ellie; if she is wrong, she must run again before she can make another guess.

> Footballers' names can be used instead, or the names of other children in the class. Younger children like to guess breakfast cereals, for example CF (corn flakes), SP (Sugar Puffs) and RK (Rice Krispies). Alternatively, the chaser can choose a new category for each round: 'This is a type of tree, beginning with B.' This variant is sometimes called *Anything under the Sun*.

GOBLIN CHASER

CODEBREAKER

(FOR 6 OR MORE PLAYERS, AGE 8+)

You will need: coloured chalks

With the chalks, the players draw a den (where the prisoners are to be held), an escape hatch (a small square approx 30 × 30 cm) adjoining the den, and finally the 'code'.

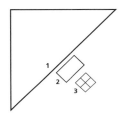

1. **Den**
2. **Escape hatch**
3. **Code**

The code is drawn right next to the escape hatch, and is made up of jumbled letters. Here are some suggestions:

Tommy is on. The other players run away. As he catches them, Tommy puts them into the den. There is no escape from here except through the escape hatch, and it will require the help of a codebreaker.

Hugh has been caught. He is in the den. He moves into the escape hatch and holds out his hand to show that he wants to be rescued. Neil comes to the rescue. He has to break the code first, and he does it by stamping his feet, spelling out the codeword by standing on each letter in turn: O–U–T.

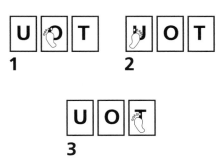

Once Neil has spelled out the letters, the code is broken. Neil touches Hugh's outstretched hand, and Hugh is free to run again.

The game is over when everyone has been caught.

- Note that the Codebreaker himself can be caught while attempting to free someone.

- Only one prisoner is allowed in the escape hatch at any one time – that is, one prisoner equals one rescuer.

- The code is not a secret. Everyone should know it before the chase begins.

- This game sounds more complicated than it actually is. Please don't feel daunted! Draw out the pitch on your own, and try spelling out the codes with your feet. Once you understand how easily it works, you will be able to demonstrate it with confidence to the children. This is a genuinely creative game – children love inventing new codes – and one that is well worth teaching.

2 × 2 ('TWO-BY-TWO')

(FOR 12 OR MORE PLAYERS, AGE 9+)

Callum is on. He tigs Tim, they join hands and chase the other players. They tig Russell, and he joins hands with them too.

> A chasing game in which chains of chasers split repeatedly into pairs.

Then they tig Ewan and *he* joins hands with them – but four is one too many! The chain must split into two pairs. Both pairs continue to chase and tig, dividing into pairs whenever a fourth person joins the chain. The game ends when everyone has been caught.

RATS AND RABBITS

(FOR 10 OR MORE PLAYERS, AGE 9+)

The players divide into two equal groups and stand in two lines, facing each other, about two metres apart. Behind each group, several metres away, there should be a back line. The caller declares one side 'rats' and the other side 'rabbits'.

A non-competitive game with (theoretically) no winners or losers, easily played on a netball court. It is a wonderful game, and one that always attracts plenty of players, but it does need adult supervision. The caller should be an adult with a loud voice, a firm hand and a large whistle!

The game begins, and the caller calls out either 'rats' or 'rabbits'.

'Rats!' she cries, and hearing this command, all the rats chase the rabbits, who run to the safe area behind their back line. Any rabbit who is caught before reaching the line is taken to join the rats.

The caller blows the whistle to bring the teams back to their starting positions. The ranks of rats have swelled visibly! The caller calls again:

'Rabbits!' and now the rabbits chase the rats, who flee to the safety of *their* back line. Again, any rat that is caught before reaching home has to join the rabbits.

The game continues, with both sides changing all the time.

• The caller does not have to follow a call for rats with one for rabbits. It can be rats–*rats*–rabbits–rats. This is why it is preferable to have an adult caller: an adult can quickly judge whether one side can withstand a second attack without the game coming to an abrupt end. Also, an adult caller is generally accepted to be impartial.

• Remember to establish the game rules before starting. Prisoners should come *willingly*; they should not fight back. No one should have their clothing pulled, and everyone must return to an orderly line when the whistle is blown.

• This is a good game for teaching children about winning, losing and the fickle finger of Fate.

RATS AND RABBITS

POLO

(FOR 4 TO 8 PLAYERS, AGE 9+)

Janie is on. She stands behind one of the lines, facing her friends, who stand behind the other line. Janie has to choose a subject for the first round. This could be fruit, drinks, pop stars, colours, types of chocolate bar… Janie decides what she wants and tells her friends: 'Colours'.

Polo is an extremely popular game with girls today. Because of this, boys will happily play it during organised games sessions, but not usually in the playground! It is a racing game, usually run between two lines on a netball court.

The other girls huddle together and decide what colours they will be. Zoe wants to be pink; Louise is purple; Rachel is gold; Kylie is green. Once they have decided, one of the girls steps forward and tells Janie the colours chosen: 'Pink, purple, gold and green.'

Janie chooses a colour from the list and shouts it out: 'Green!' Then the race begins: Janie runs across the pitch to the other line, and when she reaches it she cries 'P!' Then she runs back to her own line, where she cries 'O!' Then she runs back to the other line again, where she cries 'L!' and finally returns to her own line, where she cries 'O! POLO!'

Meanwhile, Kylie (whose colour was chosen) is doing exactly the same thing, but *in the opposite direction*.

The girl who wins the race is on for the next round and picks a new category.

SPIDER

(FOR GROUPS OF 4 TO 6, AGE 9+)

Sandeep is on. He stands a little away from the group and covers his ears. The other players decide who is going to be holding the (imaginary) spider. When they're ready, Sandeep returns to the group.

The players hold their hands behind their backs. They are pretending to be holding either a star or a spider. Sandeep has to choose someone. He chooses Victoria.

Victoria brings her hands out from behind her back, pretending that she has something small cupped in her hands. She holds her hands up close to Sandeep, opens them and says: 'Star!'

Sandeep chooses again. This time it's Glen, and he does the same thing.

Then Sandeep chooses Will. Sandeep doesn't know it, but Will has the spider! When Will opens his hands he cries out: 'Spider!' and everyone runs away.

Sandeep chases them. He tigs Glen and the game begins again, with Glen covering his ears.

- The chaser chases everyone – not just the person with the spider.

- The person who is on must keep asking the other players to show what they're holding – even if there's only one person (that is, the spider holder) left to ask! The chase can't begin until 'Spider!' is called.

JOKER IN THE PACK

(FOR 10 OR MORE PLAYERS, AGE 9+)

This is a really sophisticated game which contains a unique element: a device for bringing the game to an instant halt. The game can be played by one chaser or as a race between two chasers.

You will need: chalk

Chalk out the four suits from a pack of cards: hearts, diamonds, clubs and spades. Each of these should be large enough for one person to stand in:

Fred is on; he covers his ears while the other players decide who among them will be the Joker in the Pack. They do not reveal the identity of the Joker to Fred, but once they have chosen, the chase can begin. Fred has to catch four people, without picking the Joker, to make up a set of playing cards. If he picks the Joker, the game will instantly be over, and he will have failed.

Fred catches Pimmi and puts her on the heart symbol. Next he catches Oliver, and puts him on the diamond. Then he catches Belle and puts her on the spade… *No!* She's the Joker! Belle and the other 'cards' instantly sit down to show the game is over. Fred has been beaten, and Belle becomes the new chaser.

To play the game with two chasers, simply chalk two sets of symbols, one for each chaser. There is still only *one* Joker. The game ends either a) when one chaser completes his hand, making him a winner or b) when the Joker is picked by either chaser. In this case, *both* chasers are considered beaten. The Joker is Chaser 1 in the next round, and he decides who Chaser 2 shall be.

If a chaser manages to complete his hand, he stays on for a second round, and maybe even a third – until he is beaten.

JOKER IN THE PACK

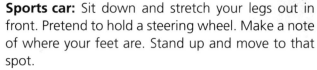

CHARLIE'S ANGELS

(FOR 5 OR MORE PLAYERS, AGE 9+)

This game for girls is an updated version of the traditional game *May I?* It is often played within the lines of a netball court, but lines aren't essential.

Mel is on. She is 'Charlie' and she stands behind one line. The other players – the Angels – line up behind another line, facing her. In strict rotation, Mel gives her friends instructions. As they carry them out, the girls move across the space between the lines. The first girl to cross Mel's line is the winner, and takes Mel's place. Before a player can move, however, she *must* say 'Thank you, Charlie'. If she forgets, she has to go right back to the beginning. For example:

MEL:	**Debbie – take two leaps in the dark.**
DEBBIE:	**Thank you, Charlie.**
(Debbie makes her move.)	
MEL:	**Toni – take a helicopter.**
TONI:	**Thank you, Charlie.**
(Toni makes her move.)	
MEL:	**Nina – take three sports cars.**
(Nina makes her move, without thanking Charlie.)	
EVERYONE:	**Aaah! You didn't thank Charlie! Back to the beginning!**

The girls can invent their own moves, but these are a start:

Helicopter: Make a twirl through 360°, with arms extended, travelling as you go. (This should take three steps.)

Sports car: Sit down and stretch your legs out in front. Pretend to hold a steering wheel. Make a note of where your feet are. Stand up and move to that spot.

Leap in the dark: Take a jump forward, with feet together and eyes closed.

Blade: A martial arts move. Go forward with one foot and a downward slice of one arm, like a blade cutting through air. Move your back foot level with your front.

Freeze: Move one foot to the side, knees bent, with arms outstretched and hands together, like you're pointing a gun. No actual forward movement.

Trapdoor: Link both your hands together and step through them.

Time zone: Take one long step *backwards*, like you've stepped into a time zone that is one hour behind.

Passport: Sit on your haunches and jump forward once.

Speedboat: Lie down on the ground, stretch out your fingers, then stand on the spot your fingers touched.

London to Paris: Charlie turns her back. Run up to Charlie (without touching her) and back to the starting line. Keep going until Charlie says stop.

Karate kick: Do a karate kick from a standing position, then move forward to where you kicked with your foot.

Mobile phone: Take a tiny step, measured by putting your heel against the toes of your other foot.

Flashlight: Move one star jump forward (with arms and legs extended).

Tightrope: Take five heel-to-toe baby steps.

Bomb: From a crouching position, take one explosive leap forward.

Prisoner: Take two jumps forward with your feet together and your arms held across your body (like you have been tied up).

Slip 'n' slide: Slide one foot forward as far as possible, then draw the other one up to it.

Super sexy: Take four steps forward with your hands on your swaying hips.

Coast to coast: Take one huge step forward, as big as you can manage.

Smokescreen: Close your eyes and walk forward until Charlie tells you to stop.

- This is a curious game. It looks competitive; the girls will scrutinise every move to make sure steps are no bigger than they should be; there *is* a winner. But Charlie controls every move, determines everyone's progress and ultimately chooses the winner. The whole game revolves around her whims – but this is why girls love it! Being Charlie is to have power, control and glamour in one heavenly package. Being an Angel means laughing at your friends' silly moves, and living in hope of being picked as Charlie. And all this is wrapped up in a glitzy, fantasy scenario, straight from the movies. Irresistible!

- Charlie is a great role for a girl with limited mobility. Or a boy: Charlie *is* male in the film, after all!

CHARLIE'S ANGELS

LIFT OFF!

(FOR 2 PLAYERS, AGE 9+)

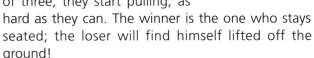
Best played on grass

The players sit on the ground opposite each other, with their feet touching (sole to sole) and holding hands. On the count of three, they start pulling, as hard as they can. The winner is the one who stays seated; the loser will find himself lifted off the ground!

QUICKSAND

(FOR 6 TO 7 PLAYERS, AGE 9+)

You might need: a piece of chalk

The 'Quicksand' is a rectangle (approx 50 × 70 cm) chalked onto the playground (or it might be possible to use a pre-painted shape). All the players join hands and then, by manoeuvring and pulling, they must try to make each other put a toe into the quicksand. When this happens, that player is out and the game continues until one player is the victor (or until just two are left, then you can call it a draw).

- The game should be about balance and tactics rather than brute force, but the players *must* be equally matched in terms of size and weight.

- If boys become too boisterous, suggest that the first player out becomes a referee. He can then step in like a boxing referee would, temporarily halting the action if, for example, one of the boys stumbles to the ground. He can then begin the game again, when everyone is on his feet and ready. He might like to use the phrase 'Time out!' (see page 64 in 'How to transform your playground').

- The players must hold hands in a joined circle at all times.

- Note that if the chalked rectangle is too large, it will be impossible for just three or four players to straddle it once others have been eliminated.

CHAPTER 3

INDOOR GAMES FOR WET PLAY

Wet playtimes are *always* unwelcome. The children want to be outside, tearing around with friends from other classes. The teachers want to be in the staffroom, savouring sweet tea and 15 minutes of peace. There's not enough time to start anything ambitious, like craftwork, and schools don't have endless supplies of art materials anyway. Then there's the problem of space…

Actually, some schools don't have this problem. They have spare halls, or empty classrooms. Some even have Dutch barns, bigger than football pitches. Bigger, in fact, than some school playgrounds! So in this chapter, I have divided the games into two groups: those that can be played in a classroom, and those that need *some* space but are still reasonably contained. Even if your class can't have use of the hall during playtime, the hall games will enliven any PE session. It's also worth remembering that all the hall games are perfectly at home on the playground too – especially on those days when it is just too hot to run around.

The games have been arranged in order of difficulty, beginning with those suitable for infants. None of the games is really *difficult*, but since classroom games exercise the brain rather than the body, other skills come into play, such as the ability to formulate and ask questions (as in *Sausages*, see page 43) or to be wildly imaginative (as in *King for the Day*, see page 42). For all those children who *don't* have rapier minds, a few minutes of guided 'thinking time' before the game begins will be very welcome. Alternatively, they can take a non-speaking role (like the guards in *King for the Day*) or they can simply watch. One of the few bonuses of indoor play is that 'sitting out' isn't regarded as anti-social; given the space constraints, it seems very *considerate* behaviour!

CLASSROOM GAMES

GRANNY'S GLASSES
(FOR 2 OR MORE PLAYERS, AGE 4+)

A sitting-down finger and wordplay game.

The (adult) leader sings the following action rhyme with the children. The children will soon learn the words themselves:

Here are Granny's glasses
(Make two circles with your hands and place them against your eyes.)
And here is Granny's hat.
(Make a triangle shape on top of your head.)
And here's the way she folds her hands
(Fold hands.)
And puts them in her lap.
(Put hands in lap.)

Here are Granddad's glasses
(Repeat action.)
And here is Granddad's hat
(Repeat action.)
And here's the way he folds his arms
(Fold arms.)
And sits like that.

GRANNY'S GLASSES

TOUCH WHAT I SAY

TOUCH WHAT I SAY
(FOR 2 OR MORE PLAYERS, AGE 4+)

The (adult) leader simply tells the children what they must touch…

Touch something *blue*… Touch something *green*… Touch something *yellow*…

…and the children must touch something appropriate, either on themselves or somewhere nearby. Begin with colours and progress to *soft, shiny, cold, hard, wooden* and so on.

WISH UPON A STAR
(FOR 6 OR MORE PLAYERS, AGE 4+)

You will need: a silver star (you could use a Christmas decoration, if you have one to hand)
The children sit in a circle on the floor, and the star is passed from hand to hand while you lead with this simple song:

This is a variation on *Pass the Parcel*. Begin by explaining the concept of wishing upon a star. In Disney's *Pinocchio*, for example, the wooden boy dreams of becoming real, and his friend Jiminy Cricket tells him to wish upon a star. People can make a wish if they see a shooting star, because it's supposed to be lucky.

A silver star
To wish upon,
Make a wish
And pass it on!

When the song stops, the child holding the star says: 'I wish… I had a puppy.' The song is repeated and the star is passed on.

- Make up a simple tune to accompany the words.

- Before you start, tell the children that they don't *have* to tell everyone their wish: it can be a secret. Infants will happily blurt out *anything*, but an older child might want to wish that her parents wouldn't get divorced, or that 'Mummy gets better'. They can simply say 'I wish for *something secret*' and then make the wish inside their head.

- This 'secret wishing' can be put to powerful use in circle time. In dark, worrying times (when there's been a national disaster, for example, or a death within the school), it gives children an opportunity to focus on their feelings and perhaps wish for a brighter future.

- Taped music can be substituted for the song.

NICE LITTLE KITTEN

(FOR 6 OR MORE PLAYERS, AGE 6+)

Everyone sits in a circle on the floor. Winston is on; he is the kitten. He sits in the middle, and his aim is to make one of the other players smile. He decides to try his luck with Adam, so he crawls up to him and starts pretending to be a kitten. He mews, he purrs, he rolls on his back, he rubs against him… Adam keeps a straight face while he strokes Winston three times, saying:

Nice little kitten. Nice little kitten. Nice little kitten.

Winston must try someone else. He chooses Sanjay, who bursts into a fit of giggles as soon as Winston starts snuffling in his ear!

Sanjay becomes the new kitten, and Winston takes his place in the circle.

NICE LITTLE KITTEN

If *everyone* is laughing, reward the child who manages to keep a straight face with the chance to be the new kitten – that is, reverse the above.

GOTCHA!

(FOR 5 OR MORE PLAYERS, AGE 6+)

You will need: a handkerchief or rag (and possibly a piece of string)
Alan is on. The handkerchief is placed in his back pocket, with a corner dangling. (If there is no pocket, use a piece of string as a makeshift belt and tuck the handkerchief into that.)

Alan stands with his back to the other players. Josie creeps up behind him, steals the handkerchief and hides it behind her back. Then all the possible thieves line up in a police identity parade, with their hands behind their backs.

Alan must try to guess the thief. He has three guesses. First, he chooses Ray; Ray shows his empty hands. Next he chooses Helen; she too shows her empty hands. Then he chooses Josie… she shows him the handkerchief and Alan instantly grabs her hands and cries out: 'Gotcha!' Because he guessed correctly, Alan stays on for another round. (If he doesn't guess correctly after three attempts, the thief is on in his place.)

BUSY BOBBY

BUSY BOBBY

(FOR 7 OR MORE PLAYERS, AGE 6+)

Maisie is on; she is Busy Bobby. She stands in front of the class (or in the middle of a standing circle, if space permits). The class begins to chant:

Busy *(Strike table or left thigh with left hand.)*
Bobby *(Strike table or right thigh with right hand.)*
What's your *(Click left-hand fingers in the air.)*
Hobby? *(Click right-hand fingers in the air.)*

They chant this four times, while Maisie begins to mime an action: driving. After the chanting stops, the first person to call out correctly what Maisie is miming becomes the new Busy Bobby.

> Note that several children might shout out answers, but it is the first correct one that Maisie *hears* who takes her place, and she may insist on precision:
> 'Driving a car?'
> 'No.'
> 'Driving a *tractor*?'
> 'Yes!'

ELECTRIC SHOCK

(FOR 10 OR MORE PLAYERS, AGE 7+)

Everyone stands in a circle, holding hands. Jerome is on; he stands in the middle of the circle. The people in the circle silently pass a pulse around the circle – that is, when someone's hand is squeezed, they squeeze the hand of the person next to them. Jerome must try to spot the squeeze as it happens. When he succeeds, the person caught making the squeeze takes his place in the middle.

> Note that there should only be one pulse going round the circle at any one time, but it can go either way – that is, you can send the squeeze back the way it came.

VICTIM

(FOR 10 OR MORE PLAYERS, AGE 7+)

You will need: a large blanket and a drum (not essential, but fun!)
Jason is on. He holds the drum while all the players stroll nonchalantly around the room. When Jason bangs the drum, everyone must fall down dead! They can lie on the floor, slump over tables or collapse in chairs – and they must *close their eyes.* Jason covers one of the victims – Iris – with the blanket, then bangs the drum again. The players gather around the blanket, and try to guess who the murder victim is. When they guess correctly, Iris emerges to great applause, and she takes the drum.

> • This is basically a junior version of *Hedgehogs* (see page 15 in 'Games for infants'), but it requires less room.
>
> • Note that the *victim* is on in the following round – *not* the person who guesses correctly. This reduces cheating, by removing any possible benefit to peeping.

KING ON HIS THRONE

POSTMAN PAT HAS LOST HIS CAT

(FOR 6 OR MORE PLAYERS, AGE 7+)

> This guessing game is a variation of *I Spy*.

Julie is on. She sits at the front of the class and says:

Postman Pat has lost his cat.
Some say this and some say that.
But I say Mr _____ stole it!

Mr _____ is a colour, for example Mr Blue, and it relates to the colour of the object Julie has chosen: a blue pencil. The other children simply have to guess the object.

> Older children may like to use a person's title as a clue, for example *Miss* Pink would be something belonging to one of the girls, but *Mrs* Brown would be something belonging to the teacher. This allows the objects to be a little more challenging, such as a buckle on a shoe.

KING FOR THE DAY

(FOR 10 OR MORE PLAYERS, AGE 8+)

The King (or Queen) sits on his 'throne' at the front of the room, flanked by two guards. One by one, all the other players approach the King and fall to their knees. Then they beg and grovel, promising all kinds of outlandish things if only the King will spare their lives:

I promise to eat everyone's leftovers at dinner time!
I promise to sweep the playground with a toothbrush.
I promise to sniff your socks after you've worn them for a week!

The King listens, and then declares: 'Off with her head!' or 'You are saved.' After sentencing, the players form two groups either side of the King. When the King has heard everyone, he calls for his guards and they escort those to be beheaded out of the room.

Once they are outside, with the door closed behind them, they pretend to scream in terror while everyone *inside* the classroom cheers!

- A wonderful game to play on someone's birthday.
- The King is a fine role for a child in a wheelchair.

THE MYSTERIOUS MR X

(FOR 8 OR MORE PLAYERS, AGE 8+)

Barry is the detective. He leaves the room while the other children decide who among them is going to be the Mysterious Mr X. Barry returns and sits at the front of the class.

> This is a guessing game in which one child is the detective while the others provide the clues.

He points at someone and asks them a question about Mr X, for example 'Is he a boy or a girl?' or 'What colour is his hair?' After each clue, Barry makes a guess. When he finally guesses correctly, it is the person who supplied that final clue who becomes the new detective.

CHICKENS FOR SALE

(FOR 6 OR MORE PLAYERS, AGE 8+)

Becky is on; she is the buyer. All the other players are chickens for sale, and they form a line, facing forwards.

The aim of this game is for the buyer to make the chickens laugh. Becky moves along the line slowly, considering each chicken in turn. She can tickle them, prod them – whatever she wants!

'I want a nice *juicy* one for my pot!' says Becky, squeezing someone's cheeks. 'This one won't do!'

If the chicken laughs (or even smiles, depending on how strict you want to be), the buyer removes it from the line. The last chicken left becomes the new buyer.

BLEEP!
(FOR 3 OR 4 PLAYERS, AGE 8+)

You will need: reading books with large, clear type (picture books are best)

> This is a game for confident readers.

Annie starts reading aloud, as fast as she can. Whenever she reaches a word beginning with the letter 's' she must say 'Bleep!' The other players listen carefully, waiting for a mistake. As soon as she says an 's' word, the book is passed on to the next player.

> To make the game harder, add another set of words to bleep out, for example 't' words. Try a bleep for an 's' word and a 'Bzzz!' for a 't' word!

ZIP ZAP BOIING
(FOR 10 OR MORE PLAYERS, AGE 8+)

Everyone stands in a circle, and one person begins by sending a *zip* to the person next to them. (A zip is a gesture like a magician's flourish accompanied by the word 'zip'.) The zip flies around the circle (clockwise or anticlockwise) with everyone doing a zip in turn.

Once everyone has got the hang of a zip, you introduce the *zap*. The zap is a blocking gesture (with the word 'zap') that sends the zip back the way it came. (Note that when it does go back the way it came, it reverts to zip–zip–zip.)

Finally, introduce the *boiing*. This allows you to send the current across the circle, with a zip-type gesture and the word 'boiing'.

> • This game is *much* easier than it sounds!
>
> • Note there should only be one current going around the circle at any one time.
>
> • This game can be played as a knockout. If a player hesitates or makes a mistake, they're out!

SAUSAGES
(FOR 5 OR MORE PLAYERS, AGE 8+)

The players form a circle, either sitting or standing. Chloe is on and she goes in the middle. The aim of the game is to make Chloe smile. One by one, going in a clockwise direction round the circle, every player asks Chloe one question. For example:

> **What do you brush your hair with?**
> **What do you wear on your feet?**
> **What are your brothers made of?**

The only answer that Chloe can give to any question is 'Sausages'. Chloe tries to keep a straight face, but as soon as she smiles, the person who asked the question that made her smile is on in Chloe's place.

> • The person in the middle must physically turn to face their questioner, and they cannot rest their chin on their hands!
>
> • Pacing is important in this game. Encourage the children to say 'pass' if they cannot think of a question.
>
> • Some children are really good at keeping a straight face! You can introduce the rule that a person can stay on for just 'once around the circle' and then they are congratulated, dismissed and allowed to choose their own successor.

> *Wizards, Giants and Dwarves* is perfect for the classroom too, when played in pairs (see page 30 in 'Games for juniors').

HALL GAMES

SLEEPING LIONS
(FOR 10 OR MORE PLAYERS, AGE 5+)

The teacher is on. All the children lie on the ground and pretend to be sleeping lions. After the count of three, no child must move a muscle. If they do, they are out of the game.

- In theory, the game continues until just one child remains, and he is the winner. In practice, however, I like to end the game when there are still half a dozen children left. I simply clap my hands and say: 'If you're still lying down, *you're a winner*! Well done!' This makes the game less competitive and more rewarding.

- If you tell the children to close their eyes, then they can't be out for blinking.

SHARKS
(FOR 10 OR MORE PLAYERS, AGE 7+)

You will need: several small PE mats
Position the mats around the hall. These are islands, and a player cannot be tigged while he is standing on one. The rest of the floor is the sea.

Gary and Gemma are on. They are the sharks, and they patrol the sea. The other players must run between the islands, but when the sharks catch them, they are turned to stone! They must sit down cross-legged on the floor, exactly where they were caught.

The game is over when everyone has been turned to stone. The last runners to be caught become the new sharks and the game begins again.

- This can be played outside, using chalk islands.

- *Sharks* is a good game for teaching the benefits of teamwork. If the sharks work co-operatively, they will catch people more easily.

DOCTOR DOLITTLE
(FOR 10 OR MORE PLAYERS, AGE 7+)

Everyone stands in a circle, holding hands. Ross stands in the middle with his eyes closed. He is Doctor Dolittle. The children walk or dance around him in their circle until he cries, 'Stop!' Then, with his eyes still closed, he points to someone in the circle and gives them the name of an animal.

'Lion!' he says. He is pointing at Elizabeth, and so she must make the noise of a lion. Ross has to guess who is making the sound. He has three guesses. If he guesses correctly, Elizabeth will become the new Doctor Dolittle. If he fails, Ross must stay on and the game begins again.

FRUIT SALAD
(FOR 12 OR MORE PLAYERS, AGE 8+)

You might need: chairs (good but not essential)
Everyone sits in a tight circle, either on the floor or on chairs. Dannii is on. She stands in the middle and thinks of three fruits. She tells the others her list: 'Apple – pear – banana' and then *she must wait* while the others mentally decide which one of these fruits they will be.

Then Dannii cries out the name of just one of the fruits: 'Banana!' and anyone who chose banana for themselves has to stand up, run into the circle and reseat themselves in a newly vacated space. Dannii tries to claim one of these spaces too, of course, and the person left standing is the next one on.

- Each new person on can choose different fruits.

- The caller always stands, even in the sitting-on-the-floor version.

- Instead of naming one of the three fruits, the caller can also cry out: 'Fruit Salad!' This means that *everyone* has to change places. Note this is really only an option when the game is played with chairs.

SPIN THE SPIDER

THE MUSCLE MACHINE
(FOR AN EVEN NUMBER OF PLAYERS, AGE 10+)

Something challenging for older juniors! This is an exercise in balance and co-operation, based on the principles behind a *yurt*: a Mongolian tent which is held up by the walls pressing against the roof. It requires a little time and good discipline, but it's very rewarding.

SPIN THE SPIDER
(FOR 7 OR MORE PLAYERS, AGE 8+)

You will need: a tin plate, with a spider painted on it

All the players sit in a circle on the floor, with one person in the middle holding the plate. Everyone (including the spinner) is given a number. Craig is in the middle. He spins the plate and calls out a number: '2!' Alastair is number 2. He must dash into the circle and catch the plate before it stops spinning. If he succeeds, everyone claps. Whether he succeeds or not, Alastair sets the plate spinning again, then calls out a new number.

Players keep the same numbers throughout the game.

Everyone stands in a circle, firmly holding hands. An adult walks around the circle, alternately naming children 'In' or 'Out'. On the count of three, all the Ins *lean in* to the circle, while the Outs *lean out*. With everyone concentrating, the circle will balance perfectly. When the children have mastered this, on the count of three the players can switch roles – that is, the Ins lean out and vice versa. Again, with concentration and slow-controlled movement, perfect balance can be achieved.

THE MUSCLE MACHINE

OTHER GAMES THAT CAN BE PLAYED (WITH CARE) IN A SMALL HALL

From 'Games for infants':
Round and Roundy! (page 13), *Bees in the Hive* (page 13), *Hedgehogs* (page 15), *Little Baby* (page 15), *Duck Duck Goose* (page 15), *Chop! Chop!* (page 19), *Five Currant Buns* (page 19), *Fishes in the Net* (page 21) and *Jelly on a Plate* (page 21).

From 'Games for juniors':
Vampire Slayer (page 27), *Blade* (page 28), *Rats and Rabbits* (page 34), *Joker in the Pack* – using four different-coloured hoops (page 35), *Charlie's Angels* (page 36), *Lift Off!* (page 37) and *Quicksand* – using a very small PE mat (page 37).

From 'Working with special needs':
Snake in the Grass (page 49).

CHAPTER 4

WORKING WITH SPECIAL NEEDS

Playground games aren't fair. They favour fast runners and quick thinkers; robust boys, who can shrug off bone-crunching collisions; sharp-witted girls, who can fire questions like gilded arrows. Playground equipment demands dexterity too: skipping with two long ropes (*Double Dutch*) is a remarkable display of hand and eye co-ordination.

In special schools, playground equipment is carefully chosen to suit the needs and abilities of the children. The adult–child ratio is higher, and so there is usually someone on duty who can organise a satisfying game or two. But what happens in a mainstream school, when there's a solitary child in a wheelchair? Does he watch from the sidelines, running with his friends in spirit only?

Well, yes and no. I am always fascinated by the dynamics of a class with a special educational needs (SEN) child. In some schools, when I lead a games workshop, children will protest on that child's behalf, saying: 'Miss, that's not *fair*! John can't do that!' But in other schools, the child will simply be incorporated into the game, without question – even if the game becomes absurd as a result! In the game *Hedgehogs*, for example, a child is concealed beneath a blanket and the others have to guess who it is. When that child is in a wheelchair, it is patently obvious who it is, but it is still taken seriously, and everyone is thrilled at the uncovering. It is heart-warming to watch.

In the playground, however, outside a workshop situation, the dynamic usually changes. Play might begin with a game that everyone can do, like *Sausages*, but then suddenly someone will cry, 'Let's play tig!' and the runners are gone, their companion apparently forgotten. No one ever seems to protest that *this* isn't fair. Curiously, even the one left behind seems to accept it, realising that such decisions are born of energy rather than malice.

USING TRADITIONAL GAMES TO EXPLORE DISABILITY AND EQUALITY

Children do not play consciously; they play spontaneously. It simply doesn't occur to them (especially gifted runners) that some games are exclusive, and while they accept that a child in a wheelchair has limitations, most offer little sympathy to those who can't run because of other problems, like obesity. It is worth challenging such insensitivity through a games workshop, using traditional games to explore issues such as equality, fairness and disability. Two useful games for this work are *Frog in the Middle* and *Jingling*. (*Note:* these are intended for supervised workshop use only, and are not recommended for general playground use.)

FROG IN THE MIDDLE

According to Iona and Peter Opie (*Children's Games in Street and Playground*, Oxford Paperbacks), this game is based on an Ancient Greek game called *Chytrinda*. There is a description of it by Pollux, dating from 1800 years ago, which describes how one boy would be the Chytra (or 'pot'). He sat on the ground, while the other boys ran around him, taunting, teasing and hitting him. When the pot managed to catch one of his tormentors, *he* became the new pot.

To play *Frog in the Middle*, divide the class into small groups of seven or eight. Each group has a chair, and the person who is on (the frog) has to sit on the chair. He cannot come off the chair but still has to attempt to tig one of the other players, who circle him. When he finally tigs someone, that person becomes the new frog.

Don't reveal too much about the game in advance, and make no mention of wheelchairs at this stage. You want the children to play *instinctively*.

It is interesting to watch the game develop. Because it's dull, boring and repetitive, many children start to spice it up to make it more interesting. Soon they are poking the frog, calling him names, pulling faces – some will even try to pull him off the chair!

After a few minutes of play, the discussion can begin. Did they enjoy the game? How did it feel to be the frog? What about their attitude and behaviour towards the frog? Now imagine that the chair was a *wheelchair*, and they really couldn't move. How would they feel then? Explore the idea of limited mobility. If a new girl joined their class, and she was in a wheelchair, would she be able to play the games they normally play? How could they be adapted to suit her needs?

BLIND MAN'S BUFF: a consideration

Now picture this. There is a new boy joining the class. He is fit and healthy, has the use of both legs and is able to run, but he still can't join in ordinary games. Why?

He is blind.

What game could you play with someone who is blind? *Blind Man's Buff*, of course! But consider the game more carefully. One person is blindfolded, spun around to disorientate them, and then they must stumble blindly on, trying to catch someone. And what exactly is a 'buff'? It's a 15th-century term to describe a blow, especially one from a fist. To 'buffet' means to knock about, or to force one's way, as through a crowd. This game clearly has a rough history!

Imagine you were *really* blind. How would you feel if your friends suggested a game like this? What other games could you play instead? You could try *Jingling*. This was very popular in Elizabethan England. At country fairs, there would be jingling contests, and the person who evaded capture for the longest would win a prize.

JINGLING

You will need: a thick blindfold for every player and some small sleigh bells

All the players are blindfolded except for one, who carries a set of bells. The players have to try to catch the jingler as he moves among them, jingling the bells occasionally and discreetly.

> This game can also become the basis for a separate session exploring the value of teamwork. The class may be divided into groups to consider developing strategies to catch the jingler, for example all holding hands and sweeping down the length of the hall.

ADAPTING GAMES FOR CHILDREN WITH SPECIAL NEEDS

I'm a great believer in letting children make their own adaptations. Teachers and classroom assistants are understandably cautious in their approach to such things, but children are bold creatures who will determine their own course! I remember working with teachers at a school for the deaf, where they wanted to adapt my games before I taught them to the children. When I suggested *Dead Man Arise!*, they were enthusiastic. They changed the rhyme to a stomping foot rhythm easily enough, but as for the children covering their heads with a blanket… *no*! All the staff agreed, the children wouldn't do that. Why? I asked. Because, they explained, the children were already playing without the aid of *one* sense. They wouldn't willingly give up another, it would be too scary. And so we agreed that when I demonstrated the game, I would pull the blanket up no further than my chin – then the Dead Man would be able to see *exactly* what was going on. Of course, when the children finally played the game, they were covering their heads within minutes and howling with the excitement of it all! The teachers were amazed.

I have seen *Twister* played with one girl in a wheelchair, with her helper pushing her furiously round the backs of the other players. I would not have believed it possible, but it was. They found a way.

Surprisingly, children who cannot use their legs are less hindered than those unable to use hands or arms. So many games feature fingers (*Poison*) or clenched fists (*Spider*) or touching someone (*Devil's Den*) or holding hands (*Rainbows*) or miming (*Little Baby*). All chasing games are based on the concept of tigging – and a tig is a touch. Children without arms are extremely vulnerable: if they fall, they cannot save themselves, so it is very difficult for them to run with other children. I remember observing one boy like this as he played alongside 30 boisterous classmates. His assistant strapped on his safety helmet and he joined in – but I did notice that he carefully kept to the fringes of the action. He only seemed to relax when we played *Hedgehogs*. Snuffling around on the floor, there was no danger of falling, and he moved vigorously, using his helmeted head as a lever. Soon he was completely immersed in the game, and when ultimately he found himself covered with the blanket, his joy was complete.

In my experience, the best type of game for a child with restricted physicality is one in which they can be in charge: asking the questions and directing the action. The game I use most is *Snake in the Grass* (see below), which is very similar to the well-known *Please Mr Crocodile*. I was wary the first time I tried it. The boy in question didn't even have a wheelchair that could be pushed: it was more like a baby walker. But was I being patronising, giving this boy the role of snake because he was physically unable to do anything else? I needn't have worried. The boy *adored* being on. Suddenly everyone was listening to *him*, doing whatever *he* wanted them to do. I asked him to choose a helper – someone to do the running for him – and he was spoilt for choice! Everyone was pleading with him to be his legs! He chose a fast friend, and the game began, with the helper changing in each round – and then his helper caught *the fastest boy in the class*. The snake turned to me, eyes shining, almost speechless with excitement.

'Oh Miss, he's the best!' he whispered gleefully, pointing at his new runner. *'They've got no chance!'*

SNAKE IN THE GRASS

(FOR 10 OR MORE PLAYERS, AGE 7+)

Esme is the Snake. She has a helper, Kenny, who chases on her behalf. The other children stand in a line, facing her. They chant:

Snake in the grass – can I pass?

Esme looks them up and down, looking for something that some of them will have, but most won't, like white socks, glasses, a hairband, brown eyes or a certain colour of clothing.

'Only if you're wearing something *green*,' says Esme.

Anyone wearing green (even if it's only a stripe on their socks) walks safely past Esme to the other side. Then Esme cries, 'Go!' and all the other players must *run* to the other side. Kenny catches Steven. Steven is the new helper, Kenny joins the others and the game begins again.

> If everyone is in school uniform, it can be difficult to find visual differences, although there are always spectacles, long/short socks, hair accessories, shoes with/without laces and so on. Try other conditions, like 'names beginning with B' or 'only if you have a sister in the school'.

OTHER GAMES

Other games which suit a questioner/helper team are:
From 'Games for infants': *Mother Hubbard* (page 17), *The Gingerbread Man* (page 19), *Five Currant Buns* (page 19) and *Jelly on a Plate* (page 21).
   From 'Games for juniors': *King of the Wind* (page 26), *Troll Tricker* (page 31), *Pop Stars* (page 32) and *Polo* (page 34).

Games in which someone can be in charge without running are:
From 'Games for juniors': *Wizards, Giants and Dwarves* (page 30), *Rats and Rabbits* (page 34) and *Charlie's Angels* (page 36).
   From 'Indoor games for wet play': *Touch What I Say* (page 38) and *King for the Day* (page 42).

Games that are wholly verbal are:
From 'Indoor games for wet play': *Postman Pat has Lost his Cat* (page 42), *King for the Day* (page 42), *Chickens for Sale* (page 42), *The Mysterious Mr X* (page 42), *Bleep!* (page 43) and *Sausages* (page 43).

Other games that might be useful are:
From 'Games for infants': *Hedgehogs* (page 15), *Chicken Run* – children with cerebral palsy who can stand but not run *love* being the lookout arch (page 17) and *Sticky Witch* – tigging from within a pot (page 18).
   From 'Indoor games for wet play': *Granny's Glasses* (page 39), *Wish upon a Star* (page 39), *Gotcha!* (page 40), *Busy Bobby* (page 41), *Electric Shock* (page 41), *Zip Zap Boiing* (page 43), *Sleeping Lions* (page 44) and *Doctor Dolittle* (page 44).

HOW TO TRANSFORM YOUR PLAYGROUND

A playground project offers endless possibilities for curriculum-linked work, from maths (calculating area) to art (painting murals) to citizenship (are the grounds a community resource?) to science and technology (designing wind chimes). Literacy skills will be exercised with making lists and devising strategies, while oral work (often neglected) will benefit enormously from group discussions and planning sessions.

Most importantly, playground transformations endure. Murals, sculptures and flowerbeds will both enhance the school environment and symbolise the *hidden* improvements that have brought greater peace and harmony for all. They are also quantifiable proof that *something was done* to raise standards; visual testimonies to your hard work. Something to show the inspectors.

If you really want to transform your playground, the first thing you must do is *talk about it!* Everyone needs to have their say – children, teachers, lunchtime supervisors, support staff, the caretaker, your PTA – *everyone*. Of these, the children's opinions are the ones that really matter, and they can be the most surprising. When adults talk about spending money on improvements for the playground, the discussion usually turns to play equipment or having special designs painted. Children, however, frequently want seats and covered areas where they can sit and chat, protected from biting winds and drizzle. They would rather have a thousand boxes of chalk than pre-painted snakes on the playground. Many, many children feel that the quality of playtime would be improved if playing football was controlled.

Once the problems have been identified, the *children* can be set the task of solving them. For example, if football is a problem, *why* is it a problem? What are the possible solutions? They might consider:
• banning it altogether
• restricting it to the summer months, when the school field becomes available
• restricting it to one part of the playground, sectioned off with cones
• restricting it to certain days of the week
• simply buying goalposts! Providing a proper target can solve the problem of flying footballs.

If the children decide that they would like landscaped grounds, they can consider ways of raising sufficient funds for the project. Could they approach a local garden centre? Would students from the nearest art college be interested in creating murals or garden sculptures? Who would do the physical work: digging flowerbeds and building walls? Could the PTA be approached?

The support of parents will almost certainly be vital for a large transformation project – and not just for fund-raising. Parents have a wide assortment of professional skills, from bricklaying to draughtsmanship, and they will often donate their services, but always remember to involve key players right from the start. *Never* base plans on assumption – even 'fantasy' plans in the classroom. If Mr Williams in the village has a JCB, for example, and his son is in Class 4, do not assume that he will be willing (or able) to help! And although it might be the *children's* idea to ask him to uproot those dead trees, it would be wiser for the head or the PTA to ask him, rather than the children writing him a letter.

But these are big plans. The children might find bullying or litter more pressing concerns, and these can be tackled without huge financial investment. Again, the children can produce their own action plans to solve such problems, and these can often be implemented with greater success than their staff-driven counterparts.

THE LUNCHTIME SUPERVISORS' ROLE

Realistically, you will never transform your playground without the active participation and support of the lunchtime supervisors. They are crucial in both promoting and sustaining a positive playground dynamic, yet frequently they are undervalued and unsupported by the teaching staff.

I have great sympathy for lunchtime supervisors. In many schools, they have a difficult job. Children instinctively realise that although the supervisors have *some* authority over them, they do not have the disciplinary power of the teachers, and so they act accordingly: flaunting rules, answering back and denying involvement in incidents. Supervisors are usually overstretched at the best of times, and because their primary role is to keep the children safe, they are often reduced to the role of prison guards, patrolling the perimeter fence and trying to mediate in disagreements.

I have worked specifically with lunchtime supervisors on many occasions, and I always ask them to air their grievances. The list is long, and often I have been the first outsider to hear their complaints; they do not feel confident enough to confront the headteacher. This is a great shame. Here are some typical views:

• They feel undervalued.
• They are overstretched. If one child needs medical attention, the others are frequently left to fend for themselves.
• They would like to play more games, but they believe they have forgotten those they used to know, and if they are playing a game they can't watch over the other children.
• When they *do* start a game, they are mobbed by dozens of children wanting to join in.
• The play equipment is more trouble than it's worth! It causes endless fights and squabbles over who should be playing with what.
And so it goes on.

Though not in *every* school. In some schools I visit, the supervisors happily play along with the children, by whom they are clearly adored. They give up their mornings to attend workshops, and they ask for copies of the game rules. They readily discuss ways in which the playground could be improved, and they share their ideas with the headteacher. Don't you want supervisors like this?!

There are some steps you can take:

PRACTICAL HELP FOR LUNCHTIME SUPERVISORS

RAISING SELF-ESTEEM

Are they undervalued? Lunchtime supervisors spend more playing time with the children than many teachers. They have amassed hours of observation; they know what they are talking about. So listen to them! Involve them in any debate about the playground, and encourage them to voice their concerns. Ask them how you can help make their job easier, especially in terms of encouraging play. Would they like more game ideas? Lend them this book! Would they like a play specialist to do some training with them? (Incidentally, it is not a good idea to bring in a specialist without first consulting the supervisors. It can be mistaken for criticism: 'Does he think we're not doing enough?')

High self-esteem is linked to the firm belief that others respect you. I said earlier that children can instinctively feel that supervisors don't have the same authority as teachers, and behave accordingly. Supervisors want and, more importantly, *need* the respect of the children to do their job. For children to respect them, they must see that the supervisors have the respect of the teaching staff. If the supervisors have their coffee in a broom cupboard, it does not suggest that they are respected. Now it's not for me to tell you how to manage the social hierarchy of your school, so I simply *make the observation* that schools with a welcoming headteacher and a friendly staffroom open to all – teachers, visitors, support staff and supervisors alike – usually have good-natured playgrounds with an enthusiastic regard for games!

One way of raising self-esteem is to promote individuals as 'play experts'. Lunchtime supervisors are usually golden repositories of playground lore. They just don't know it! They will swear they have forgotten all the skipping rhymes they used to know, but if you actively encourage debate – over coffee, with the teachers – the memories will start to surface. Willing supervisors can wear badges saying 'Skipping expert – ask me!' and children can be encouraged to approach them for ideas and instruction.

LAMINATED CARDS

I have a box of laminated A4 game cards. On one side, there's a picture and the name of the game. On the other side, there are rules and instructions, all in child-friendly language. They are weather proof, virtually indestructible and they are indispensable. If your supervisors have a box of these to hand, they can suggest to any bored children that they play a game from the box, and there is no problem remembering how it's played.

PAINTED CIRCLES

Anyone who has ever tried to gather children (especially infants) into a circle, with everyone holding hands, will know how frustrating and time-consuming it can be. There is a wonderfully easy solution: a set of concentric circles painted onto the playground. The circles should be various sizes and different colours. For example, the smallest circle could be blue, and fit up to twenty players, and beyond that, a yellow one large enough to accommodate a whole class. When a supervisor decides to lead a game like *Wake up, Sleepy Head!* (see page 16), she simply chooses the size she will need to accommodate all the participating children, and instructs them to stand on that particular circle. Within seconds, everyone is neatly spaced, holding hands and ready to play.

THE BIG RED TOMATO CARD

Make a small laminated card (A6 size) that shows a big red tomato. This can be carried and used by anyone on playground duty. The Big Red Tomato card is a discipline aid. It's the equivalent of a yellow card in football – that is, it's a warning card, used when a player has been seen playing unfairly.

Some children can really spoil a good game and cause endless arguments. They are children who:
• chase their best friends all the time, or only chase members of their own sex
• deliberately try to get caught, usually by not running away or running slowly across the path of the person who is on.

It's from this second group of people that the Big Red Tomato card gets its name. These people are like tomatoes: they just hang around waiting to be picked! But the card can be used for all kinds of cheating and bad play.

To use the card, simply march up to the offender and with a stern but semi-comic expression on your face, waggle the card in front of their nose! Nothing needs to be said; this is the beauty of using the card. Once the children know what it means, it becomes a silent code. They know so-and-so has been out of order. They know you spotted it. They know you're not turning a blind eye to unacceptable behaviour. They know you're giving a warning. And it is just a warning. The offender is not out of the game, or sent to the sidelines; they're *under observation*.

A STRATEGY

If an overstretched supervisor finds herself caught off guard by a demanding child who wants her to play a game, she might find this strategy useful. She can simply say: 'We can play a game when you bring me *ten people* to play it.' This buys time to think while the child is finding nine other players, and sometimes it will take so long to find the other players that the bell will go before they manage it!

Incidentally, some local education authorities are finally realising that lunchtime supervisors would benefit from training. Courses are now available up to NVQ level, covering not only control and discipline issues, but also first aid and playground games. If this training isn't available in your area, it is worth asking for it. Demand creates supply!

WHOLE-SCHOOL STRATEGIES

Glance out of the staffroom window at playtime, and what do you see? Children playing together, giving a reassuring impression that they are enjoying a wealth of games. Closer inspection, however, usually reveals the opposite to be true. Many are playing an endless round of tig, occasionally spiced up into a violent variant. Some have dispensed with games altogether in favour of football. Others aren't playing at all; they're too busy eating! But I don't believe that children behave this way through choice. I have questioned hundreds of children about their use of playtime, and I have discovered that they are limited by their lack of knowledge, rather than any inherent laziness. They lack a games repertoire, and because they don't understand how games are constructed, they find it difficult to invent new ones. The ability to create new games is crucial to long-term vibrancy in the playground. Children have a voracious appetite for games. They will play a game obsessively every day for a week – and then it's dropped, like a toy after Christmas. They want something new again. Something that will excite them for another week. Old favourites will return eventually, but in the meantime the children need to devise new games: fast, furious, challenging games that they will really want to play.

Games *must* be challenging and age appropriate if they are going to generate any enthusiasm for play. Whenever I introduce myself to a class of strapping eleven-year-old lads, I see the scepticism and dismissal in their eyes. They are *too old* for playground games. All that holding hands and skipping round in circles nonsense! I tell them that some of the games will be physically demanding, but still they don't believe me. Then they play *Twister*, and after five minutes they're exhausted but grinning from ear to ear because they've enjoyed it so much.

So what follows are some simple ideas to help you generate a fresh enthusiasm for games in your playground, and my own Secret Game Formula, which will equip your children with everything they need to know to create endless new games of their own.

GAME OF THE WEEK

Each week, a new game is introduced to the school in assembly. The game is promoted by two or three children who have devised it or been taught it (by parents, perhaps, or friends in another school). The game has been seen and approved by their class teacher.

The children demonstrate the game. They explain the rules, and make a poster of them to be displayed in the hall throughout the week. The children are also given large badges to wear at playtime: 'Ask me!' or 'Game expert'. The children spend that week's playtime actively promoting the game, and they ensure that the rules are followed. They also mediate in any disagreements arising from the game. At the end of the week, they produce a smaller illustrated description of the game and its rules, which is pasted into a school games book, along with their names and the date.

SCHOOL OR CLASS PROJECT

It is the year 3000, and archaeologists have discovered a hopscotch pitch buried deep underground. What on earth was it used for?!

The children write a short play to explore this idea.

GAMES THROUGH THE AGES

Many of the games still played today are Victorian. Which ones? What games did Elizabethan children play? (See *Jingling* on page 48 in 'Working with special needs'.) What did Roman children play? Or Greeks?

What kind of games will children play in the future? Say, in 100 years' time? Will they still have playgrounds? Will children still go to school?!

Iona and Peter Opie's excellent book *Children's Games in Street and Playground* (Oxford Paperbacks) will provide many answers.

HOW TO CREATE NEW GAMES
THE SECRET GAME FORMULA

> A two-hour workshop for juniors, age 8+

If you are serious about promoting playground games, this is a wonderful formula to teach your children. Once they understand it, they will be able to create endless new games. It doesn't matter if these 'new' games are simply variants of ones they already know; it doesn't matter if they play them for only one day. What *is* important is that:

• The children were able to occupy themselves creatively.
• They actually *chose* to do so, for pleasure.
• They applied a formula to a series of random thoughts, and experimented with the results until the game actually worked.
• They worked co-operatively to achieve all this.

Clearly, a formula that can produce these kinds of results is worth investing in! It costs nothing but time: about two hours. This could be spread over two PE lessons, but ideally it should be one concentrated session *in the school hall.* (The children will need to listen, concentrate and think, and this is always difficult outside.)

I devised the formula after studying dozens of traditional games. I had often wondered if games contained a common structure. Well, they do.

All playground games contain some of the following:

1. **a good name**
2. **someone who is on**
3. **a suspense start**
4. **special words**
5. **a chase**
6. **questions and answers**
7. **teams or sides**
8. **a den**
9. **people being taken prisoner**
10. **people being rescued**

11. something happening to the prisoners
12. a way for the game to begin again
13. something spooky, supernatural, magical or 'out of this world'.

Here is a full explanation of the thirteen elements:

A GOOD NAME

Would you like to play *Triangle Tig*? No? How about *Twister*? Give a game an exciting name and it's much easier to whip up enthusiasm for it. It must sound modern too. Old-fashioned games like *I Sent a Letter to My Love* and *Farmer, Farmer, May We Cross Your Golden River?* are still as popular today as *Duck Duck Goose* (see page 15) and *Snake in the Grass* (see page 49). They have simply been updated and renamed.

SOMEONE WHO IS ON

This is the person who does the chasing, or is the focus of attention. Some children *adore* being on. For a few minutes, they have the power to control the lives of others. Other children (slower runners or shy ones) loathe it. The way to keep *everyone* happy is to choose games in which the person who is on changes all the time, like *Sick Dog* (see page 26). In games like *Rainbows* (see page 17) and *Tunnel Tig* (see page 20), in which the aim is for one person to immobilise everyone else, extra chasers will make being on less exhausting. A fair ratio of chasers to runners (or pairs of runners) in games like these is 1:10.

A SUSPENSE START

With a suspense start, only the chaser knows when the chase is about to begin. Until that moment, the runners are held in suspense, through a ritualistic use of words and movement, for example creeping forward and asking, 'What's the time, Mr Wolf?'

Games with a suspense start include *Poison* (see page 28), *Blade* (see page 28) and *Dead Man Arise!* (see page 25).

Suspense starts add tension and excitement to a game. They are also popular with slower runners; the extra seconds gained and the closer proximity of the runners makes it easier for the chaser, and introduces luck (rather than plain speed) into the equation.

Some games have a *delayed* start, rather than a suspense start, but the difference is so slight that it is not worth mentioning to children – it will only confuse them. The difference is that a delayed start has a predictable preliminary ritual; it is the same every time, and it is beyond the control of the chaser. In *Devil's Den* (see page 31), for example, all the runners know that the chase will begin as soon as they finish counting to ten. In *Spider* (see page 35), the chase will begin as soon as the spider has been found.

Other games with a delayed start include *Big Tree* (see page 14) and *King of the Wind* (see page 26).

SPECIAL WORDS
Any chant, rhyme or song that features in a game, for example 'Wake up, Sleepy Head!'

A CHASE
Seen by many children as *the* most important element in a game.

QUESTIONS AND ANSWERS
Basically a type of suspense start, but they can become the entire raison d'être for the game, especially with girls, who can be passionately interested in what everyone else is wearing (*Snake in the Grass*, see page 49) or what chocolate bar they should be (*Polo*, see page 34). The chase element exists only to determine who will wield the power in the next round.

Many of these games have a formal arrangement, with the questioner facing friends who are standing behind a line. This is a reminder of their street origins, when kerbs would mark the boundaries.

Other question-and-answer games include *Pop Stars* (see page 32) and *Jelly on a Plate* (see page 21).

TEAMS OR SIDES
'Teams' is a sports term; 'sides' would be the norm in the playground, with all its clannish connotations. But a side may consist of just one player, as in *Wizards, Giants and Dwarves* (see page 30).

A DEN
A safe zone, usually with defined boundaries, where runners cannot be tigged. Also confusingly used to describe the place where prisoners are held during a game, as in *Codebreaker* (see page 33).

PEOPLE BEING TAKEN PRISONER
Runners may be physically caught and taken to a designated area (as in *Sticky Witch*, see page 18) or simply immobilised (as in *Jack Frost and the Sun*, see page 26).

PEOPLE BEING RESCUED

This might mean a rescuer assailing the prison and releasing one or all of the prisoners, or it may mean releasing people who have been immobilised by performing an action (see *Rainbows*, page 17). In both instances, the rescuer would usually be required to shout something or perform an action to legitimise the release. It is a brave endeavour: the rescuer is not immune from being caught during a rescue attempt.

SOMETHING HAPPENING TO THE PRISONERS

The 'something' happens once everyone has been caught. Generally the prisoners come to an unhappy end, but the violence is imagined rather than acted out (see *Sticky Witch*, page 18, and *Mummy Hunt*, page 25).

A WAY FOR THE GAME TO BEGIN AGAIN

The game doesn't end as soon as one person is tigged. Instead, the person who is caught becomes the new chaser. In theory, this fluidity keeps the game exciting and everyone has a fair share of the fun. In reality, the game may be monopolised by certain individuals (see 'Troubleshooting', page 68) but this can be said of all game formats. In a game in which everyone has to be caught, it is usually the last person to be caught who becomes the new chaser.

SOMETHING SPOOKY, SUPERNATURAL, MAGICAL OR 'OUT OF THIS WORLD'

This may be anything from fantasy chasers (zombies, witches, robots) to simple 'horror' elements, like poison or spiders. These flavourings add zest to the most elementary games, and keep the interest of older children who would otherwise consider themselves too old for games.

Games with this element include *The Golden Pot* (see page 20), *Dead Man Arise!* (see page 25), *Poison* (see page 28), *Zombie Pit* (see page 30), *Wizards, Giants and Dwarves* (see page 30), *Devil's Den* (see page 31), *Spider* (see page 35) and *Snake in the Grass* – it's a talking snake! (see page 49).

HOW TO TEACH CHILDREN THE SECRET GAME FORMULA

You will need: the formula, written clearly on a piece of card or on a wipe board (keep it covered at the beginning to make it more intriguing), photocopied memory game sheets and pens (optional)

Remember that two hours should be allocated to make sure the children really understand how the formula works. If they don't understand it, they will never use it.

FIRST HOUR

First of all, talk enticingly about a secret formula that can unlock the mysteries of the playground! Then explain what a formula is. I explain it like this:

In this hour, children learn the formula and play five traditional games to see it in action.

There are all kinds of games played in the playground, and they all *seem* very different, but they're not. They all contain a *secret formula*. It's like a code. And once you've cracked the code, you can use it to create as many new games as you want.

A formula is like a skeleton. We all look very different. I have red hair; Jenny has blonde hair. I have blue eyes; Sam has brown. But underneath, our skeletons are the same. And it's like that with games too. They may *appear* to be different, but they're not. So let's look at this Secret Game Formula…

Reveal the secret formula and explain what all the elements mean, giving examples from games the children already know. Then explain that instead of just *talking* about the formula, you want them to play some traditional games so they can see it in action. Play *Sick Dog*, followed by a few more games (see box left).

Now they have seen the formula at work. In the second half, they will begin using it to make up some brand new games that have *never been played before*.

- Play *Sick Dog*, a good introductory game (see page 26), for a few minutes, then call the children back to the board and ask them what elements of the formula were in it. (There are four: a good name, someone who is on, a chase, and a way for the game to begin again.) Now they can see that even a simple game contains several elements from the formula.

- Repeat with *Poison* (see page 28). This introduces the children to the suspense start (plus a good name, someone is on, a chase, a way for the game to begin again, special words and something spooky). *Poison* is also a perfect example of a Red Star game (see page 63).

- Repeat with *Sticky Witch* (see page 18), using PE mats instead of chalk circles for the glue pots. This game introduces the prisoner elements. It's nice to *trick* the children with this game, by appearing to offer them a choice. Which game would they prefer to play next: *Sticky Witch* or *Glue Pots*? Take a vote. Then reveal that they are exactly the same game! This shows just how important a good name is. If you walked around the playground asking for people to play *Glue Pots*, you would have *x* number of players. But if you called it *Sticky Witch*, you would have *y* number of players! So, you must give your games really good names.

- Repeat with *Snake in the Grass* (see page 49), which introduces the question-and-answer element.

- Repeat with *Wizards, Giants and Dwarves* (see page 30), which introduces teams and sides.

SECOND HOUR

For your first game, keep it simple and work with the whole class. Choose just three or four elements to work with. I suggest:

- someone who is on
- a chase
- something spooky
- a way for the game to begin again.

In this hour, the children begin using the formula.

Encourage the children to think in terms of character, for example a mummy could be chasing archaeologists. Once the mummy tigs an archaeologist, that person becomes the new mummy.

Play the game for a few minutes, then gather the children together and start adding other elements, like movement. How must the mummy move? What must he do to catch an archaeologist? Perhaps he could tig her with both hands on the archaeologist's shoulders.

Add a suspense start. Perhaps the archaeologists have to wake up the mummy by chanting an ancient spell. What could the spell be?

Play it again with these additions, choose a good name, and that's it! A brand new game in minutes!

Now split the children into small working groups (preferably of their own choosing) and set them the challenge of devising a game of their own, using the formula. After 15 minutes or so, the groups demonstrate their new games.

Time permitting, the lesson can end with a memory game. First of all, *cover the formula*! Then give each group a pen and the photocopied memory game sheets that simply say 'How much of the Secret Game Formula can YOU remember?' with the numbers 1 to 13 written vertically down the side. The children must race to be the first group to remember all thirteen elements.

- Don't worry if the first 'new' game bears a marked resemblance to one of the traditional games. This doesn't make the game any less exciting for the children, and at least it shows that they have been listening, have absorbed the formula and are using it. Originality will come later.

- Avoid using the den element and/or the people-are-taken-prisoner-but-can-be-released scenario with large groups! It is generally unworkable with groups of more than ten, and needs careful consideration (see *Codebreaker*, page 33).

- Remember: the best games are generally simple in their structure with a strong theme and exciting embellishments.

THE BENEFITS OF USING A FORMULA

Why use a formula at all? Doesn't it work against spontaneity and stifle creativity?

In my experience, no! It doesn't. On the contrary, it gives children the knowledge they need to start creating games, and it unlocks their imaginations. The formula is merely a skeleton; the children flesh its bones. It is true that many of the games will be variations on games they already know, and also true that most won't last longer than a single playtime. But my aim here is simply to encourage children to use their playtime creatively, exercising both their brains and their bodies, and the formula does support that aim. It doesn't matter if a game is played only once, 15 minutes have been put to positive use, and the children have worked co-operatively. Even the most popular games fall in and out of favour, along with trends for skipping, yo-yos and the latest collectable. Children are interested in something that is new and fresh, and the formula is perfect for creating instant, throwaway games – and perhaps a couple that will live on to be the next generation's classics.

Here is a fine example of a game devised using the Secret Game Formula. It was created by a mixed class of seven- to eleven-year-olds at St John the Baptist Primary School, Ruyton XI Towns, near Shrewsbury.

MONSTER'S BREAKFAST

(FOR 10 OR MORE PLAYERS, AGE 8+)

The chaser is a six-eyed monster. He chases cornflakes, who must run in a semi-squatting position with their hands on their knees (sumo style). When they have been tigged, the cornflakes huddle together in an imaginary bowl. Once everyone has been caught, the monster turns his back and starts an elimination process.

'Keep standing only if you are wearing white socks,' he commands. 'Keep standing only if you have dark hair.'

When only one person is left standing (the cornflakes tell him when), the monster turns around, cries 'Milk! Milk!' and imaginary milk pours down from the heavens onto the cornflakes, turning them to mush. The person who was left standing after the elimination becomes the new monster.

This game contains an astonishing *ten* elements, but the top honours must go to the village school in Llanellen, Monmouthshire, where the single class of juniors managed to include all thirteen elements *and* a fourteenth element so sophisticated I couldn't wait to use it myself! (I have incorporated it into *Joker in the Pack* in 'Games for juniors', page 35.)

RED STAR GAMES

There is another major benefit to be gained from the Secret Game Formula workshop. Since the children will be creating brand new games, it is a perfect opportunity to encourage them to create exactly the kind of games you want to see in your playground. What are the criteria for a good game? Once these are agreed, you can decide to award special status to any games (new or otherwise) that meet the required standard. I call such games 'Red Star games', and my list is as follows.

A Red Star game must be:
- **exciting, stimulating, challenging, skilful and creative**
- **open to everyone who wants to play**
- **played by the rules.**

A Red Star game must not:
- **hurt the people playing it**
- **make it dangerous for other people in the playground**
- **take up all the available space**
- **make fun of other people.**

A list like this not only provides the opportunity to discuss several important playground issues (verbal bullying, physical safety, responsible play, the importance of rules, the need to share). It also helps children to understand why some games (namely *British Bulldog*) are unacceptable. The teachers are not simply being spoilsports, there are good reasons why it can't be played.

If you have a school games book (see 'Game of the week' on page 55), remember to paste a big red star next to these specially approved games. I also reward game inventors with a Red Star game award certificate. This is easily designed on a computer (see above).

These certificates can be framed, presented during assembly and finally displayed in a prominent position.

RED STAR GAME AWARD

Presented to
_____
for creating the game

_____

_____

Date _____

Signed _____
(Headteacher)

TIME OUT!
A SELF-HELP STRATEGY FOR CHILDREN

This is essential for physical games like *Quicksand* (see page 37), but equally useful for all children as a means of protecting themselves against physical injury. By calling a temporary halt to the game, it allows a player to moderate his friends' dangerous antics in a readily acceptable way.

The line between 'boisterous' and 'dangerous' is easily crossed. Many children don't care when it happens; some deliberately encourage it, but for others it can be a scary situation. Suddenly the game is spiralling out of control… clothes are being torn, kicks are being aimed, fists are flying, someone's fallen… it's not funny any more. But how do you make everyone stop without being called a sissy?

Calling 'Time out!' is the simple solution. It's a phrase most children will recognise from watching sport on television, especially ice hockey and American football. It means 'Stop what you're doing *now*' and it gives everyone a chance to calm down, catch their breath and appraise the situation. Perhaps someone has fallen. Perhaps someone is hurt. Perhaps someone is seriously out of breath. Perhaps it *was* getting a bit wild!

It is important that the children understand that as a command, 'Time out!' must be obeyed – instantly. And it's *serious*; it's not a jokey thing to call out just to avoid being tigged. Remember the story of the boy who cried wolf?

BARLEY! MORE SELF-HELP FOR CHILDREN

Another useful word to introduce into the playground vocabulary is 'Barley'. This is an old term, much used in my youth, that means 'Go away! I'm out of the game right now. Choose someone else!'. There will be a good reason for calling barley, such as losing a shoe during a chase, having to tie shoelaces, or genuinely needing to catch your breath. The player is quite happy for the game to continue, but he is temporarily out of play.

'Barley' can also be used to claim immunity during a tigging game, when conditions have been met. For example, in *Huggy Bear Tig* (see page 17) a player cannot be tigged if she is hugging someone, so if a girl is being chased, she might grab a friend and cry 'Barley!' just as the chaser tries to tig her.

There is a game called *Barley* that is perfect for introducing this concept.

BARLEY
(FOR 6 OR MORE PLAYERS, AGE 7+)

Zhang is on. All the players, including Zhang, crouch down in a close circle with one hand touching the ground. They chant:

Red you're dead
Blue you're true
Green you're mean
But barley is –

'Yellow!' cries Zhang. Everyone leaps to their feet and the chase begins. Zhang cannot tig anyone who is touching yellow: a yellow litter bin, perhaps, or a yellow stripe on a sweater. Zhang tigs Elspeth, and the circle forms again, with Elspeth choosing a new colour for barley.

- Even though red, blue and green are mentioned in the rhyme, they can still be used for barley.

- It's a good idea to rule that players cannot hold onto the clothes of people *not* playing the game. This prevents infants in lime green coats being unexpectedly grabbed by half a dozen juniors!

- If all the runners find barley before the chaser has tigged someone, the chaser must declare himself beaten and recall the players into the circle. He chooses again – this time something harder, like pink or purple. Barley doesn't have to be a colour. It can be wood, metal or glass. Or a shape, like a circle.

CHAPTER 6

TROUBLESHOOTING

Do you have tiny despots dominating your playground and defying your lunchtime supervisors? Do you have boys who seem incapable of playing sensibly? Do you have girls who won't play anything at all? Does the staffroom corridor turn into a casualty ward every playtime?

If so, you're not alone! Across the country, schools face the same problems, and to be honest, they are extremely difficult to solve. Playgrounds, after all, are a reflection of society. Children go out to play armed with experience: everything they have ever seen on television or at the cinema; everything they have ever heard at home, good or bad; everything they have ever been told by their friends, and by older children, about the world and its ways, and what you must do to survive. It's all there, carried on their shoulders like rucksacks, weighting every action. It is widely accepted that one of the functions of play is that it allows children to explore various aspects of adult life – gender roles, making a living, facing death. It also allows them to find a place in 'society', as represented by the playground. And if modern society is fuelled by self-interest, desperation, racial intolerance and the quest for physical perfection, there is little hope for peace at playtime.

All too often, the prevailing playground ethic is 'might is right'. The fastest, the strongest, the funniest, the prettiest, the naughtiest… all these will have power and status in the playground – and in the classroom, because the two can never be separated. Unfortunately, being the *cleverest* usually brings neither of these things, unless it can be combined with one of the other titles. The playground becomes an arena, and games may be used to decide these issues. It's also a place where personal needs can be exercised: the need to dominate others; the need for acceptance; the need to be the centre of attention. These needs, of course, will be present all the time, not just at playtime. A child who feels the need to dominate will seize any opportunity that presents itself, from group work in class to watching television with friends, and a sustained approach will be needed to solve the problem. Teachers are always disappointed when I tell them this! I wish I had quick and easy solutions, but I don't. Poor playground behaviour is merely the *symptom* of an underlying problem, either at home or at school, and I cannot hope to solve that; it's unique and multi-causal. I *can* however, ease the symptoms, and while that isn't solving the problem, it will make life easier for other children.

Here are the questions I am most frequently asked.

Q Some of the children are so rough. How can I stop this?

You have to appeal to their self-interest. It's a sad indication of how most modern children are, but it's true nonetheless. An insolent 'What's in it for me?' attitude prevails, despite all attempts to promote a caring, sharing ethos. It is championed by aggressive marketing, which tells everyone that they should have whatever they want, because they are special: they *deserve* it. It is supported at home, by parents who make their children believe that they are the most important person in school; other children and teachers are mere acolytes. It is bolstered through fear: the arrogant youth smoking on the train won't stop because he would gain nothing; the other passengers suffer in silence because he might turn violent if challenged. Sadly, they have been forced to adopt the same attitude, and the answer has a chilling resonance.

So, to return to the problem of rough play, the best approach is to threaten future happiness and glory. It works like this. Children who enjoy rough, physical games tend to be sporty. They like football, rugby, swimming and running. Perhaps they dream of being a professional footballer. Perhaps they would like to run in a marathon one day. They will need to be fit and strong. But ask them to imagine this:

One day you're playing a game – *British Bulldog!* – and it all gets a bit wild. Suddenly you've fallen. You've broken your leg, and it's really bad. You're in hospital for weeks, and as for the cup game – forget it! The team play without you. When you finally come out of hospital, and have the plaster cast off, you start playing again. But it hasn't mended properly, and one day, you're down again. And this time, the doctor tells you that you won't be able to play football *ever* again. And that all happened because you were daft for five minutes in the playground.

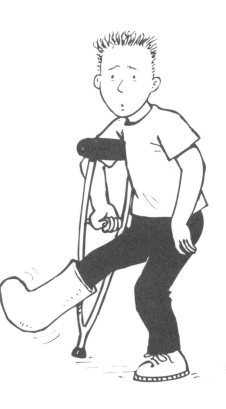

This does sound far-fetched, but it could happen. Even if you don't dream of being a professional footballer, a really bad break could mean that as an adult, you won't be able to do anything physical, like squash or badminton, rock climbing or diving, cycling or fencing. Really, would it be worth it? For the sake of a stupid game?

Tell them that they must look after themselves. They must take responsibility for their own safety. Introduce them to the 'Time out!' device (see 'How to transform your playground', page 64) and encourage them to use it.

The more personal you can make this pep talk, the more effective it will be. Fit the sport to the boy, and use what you know: 'That would be such a shame, John, wouldn't it? If you couldn't run in the London Marathon with your dad?'

Q Some of the children deliberately try to be tigged. How can I stop them doing this?

You can't! Some children *adore* being on. For a few precious minutes, they can be the centre of attention, and they will do *anything* to achieve that. Sometimes they will do things that are downright dangerous, like slowly running across the path of a speeding chaser. Culprits generally believe that no one notices these tactics, but they are glaringly obvious to any adult observer (and to many children). The best solution is to use the Big Red Tomato card (see 'How to transform your playground', page 54). It is a good idea to explain the concept first, and then to play a game that really does bring out the red tomato in people, like *Dead Man Arise!* (see page 25). It is important to make it clear that being shown the Big Red Tomato card is nothing to be proud of, otherwise some boys will use it to win 'naughtiest boy' status!

These children would also benefit from the 'Why you should play fair' speech (see page 77).

Q The children are so competitive! They are obsessed with winning and losing. Can anything be done?

This is a symptom of the 'winning at all costs' mentality. Money matters in this world, and nearly everyone dreams of winning it! Lotteries, scratch cards, bingo, television quiz shows: it's everywhere, and big winners become celebrities overnight. Increasingly, the most common taunt in playgrounds is 'loser' and I have heard it delivered with astonishing venom. It comes with a sneer of utter disdain, or with a chant and the latest 'winning mime' (those exuberant actions that footballers indulge in after scoring a goal).

There has been a trend in recent years for promoting non-competitive games, but it is an uphill struggle. Children like the element of competition, and if it isn't there, they will introduce it! The game I usually play to show children that games can be non-competitive is *Rats and Rabbits* (see page 34). Since the team members change with every round, there cannot be a 'winning team' – or so I thought. But at one school, I blew my whistle and the Rats instantly erupted into cheers and taunts. I took one of the boys aside and asked him why he felt they were winners.

'*Because*,' he explained, 'there are more rats than rabbits.'

'But if we had played another round,' I said, 'I *could* have called out "Rabbits!" and then there would have been more rabbits than rats.'

'Ah, but *when you blew the whistle* there were more rats,' he grinned. 'So we're the winners!'

Even in *Sausages* (see page 43), an extremely popular non-competitive game, there is the suggestion that the person who is on is in competition with those who are trying to make him laugh. Therefore, if he manages to keep a straight face and complete a whole circuit, he has beaten them. He's a winner!

It is extremely difficult to curb children's desire to win. It is deeply ingrained, sometimes to the point of compulsion. But you can tackle the post-game taunting.

Children never seem to think beyond the moment. They have very little concept of *consequences*. They simply don't realise that chanting 'Winner! Winner! *Loser! Loser!*' will seriously scupper their chances of a follow-on game, and could lead to a physical fight. It is worth pointing this out to them. Again, it's an appeal to their self-interest.

It is easiest to talk about this when the children can actually see it happening. If a class is prone to this kind of behaviour, it can be 'stage managed' during a PE class. *Wizards, Giants and Dwarves* (see page 30) is the best game to use, played as a whole class, boys against girls. Play the game on a 'first-team-to-five basis wins'. Stir up some tribal tension, and when this is released at the end, the euphoric winners will almost certainly begin to brag and taunt. *Now* you can step in and talk consequences.

> **Just *look* at you! What *are* you doing?! Sit down. Let's talk about this.**
>
> It is wonderful to win; it's a great feeling. If you lose – it's not so nice. But what is worse than losing is having your nose rubbed in it by the winners! That is just *horrible*. And what happens then? The losers start to sulk and get angry… I could see some of you boys just now, starting to get rattled. And I don't blame you. *I'd* get angry if the girls were winding me up like that! But if it goes on… Well, before you know it, there's a fight.
>
> And all the fun we were having… it's gone. Gone! In an instant. The boys don't want to play with you now. If you girls had just congratulated each other, and then suggested another game, we would all be playing now. And don't forget: if we had played 'first-team-to-*ten*-wins', the boys might have won. And then *you* would be the losers. Think about that!
>
> Games are supposed to be fun. That's why we play them. Have you ever heard the expression 'It's only a game'? It's true! Sometimes you win, sometimes you lose; but it's only a game, and it's not worth fighting about. It's not worth losing your friends over. So no more bragging, eh? I'll be watching you! Let's play another game…

Remember also to promote non-competitive games, perhaps as your game of the week (see 'How to transform your playground', page 55).

Q The boys play nothing but football, and the girls won't play anything at all. How can we make them more enthusiastic about playground games?

In many junior playgrounds, the boys play football while the girls huddle in corners. Now change this sentence around, and the playground starts to look different: the girls huddle in corners *while the boys play football*. If the boys weren't playing football, perhaps the girls would venture out of their corners.

Football seems to cause more problems in the playground than anything else! Boys usually play it because a) they love it, b) they don't know any good alternative games, and c) they are *allowed* to play it. Of course, they love it! It has everything they want in a game: it's fast, furious, physical, competitive, and played with friends. Playing it connects them to a multi-million dollar, global phenomenon, and just for a few minutes they can be their favourite hero. Heady stuff!

The trouble is, football takes up a lot of room. Footballs fly through the air while boys (and increasingly girls) speed after them, their eyes seeing only the goal – not the infant who has wandered into their path. If the girls *do* attempt to join in, they can find themselves mocked for their lack of skill (which is generally not a lack of skill at all, but rather a lack of

practice. How many dads encourage their baby daughters to play football?) or they find that it's too rough and dirty for their liking. (Which isn't to say that girls don't enjoy a bit of rough play! They do, but they tend to prefer it all-girls-together.)

Given the choice between football and games, boys will invariably choose football, so to encourage playground games, football must be either restricted or banned altogether. Then, seriously good alternatives must be promoted: games like *Twister* (see page 29) and *Devil's Den* (see page 31). Finally, the boys must be encouraged to make up new games and expand their repertoire. Using the 'game of the week' and Secret Game Formula strategies (see 'How to transform your playground', pages 55 and 56) can help here.

Encouraging girls to play isn't too difficult, as long as they are the right kind of games. Generally speaking, girls prefer games with a verbal element. They like questions and answers; secrets and silliness. Games like *Polo* (see page 34), *Pop Stars* (see page 32) and *Charlie's Angels* (see page 36) all fit this bill.

Older children may be reluctant to play simply because it isn't 'cool'. Playing is for kids, and they are desperate to grow up. They will happily embrace *adult* pursuits. If you were trying to encourage smoking in the playground, there would be boundless enthusiasm! But playground games? Adults don't play them. Secondary school kids don't play them. Why not? If they're such *good fun*?

Lack of opportunity, that's why! Adults love playing games – on the beach, at parties, in teacher training sessions! – but children overlook this, because they don't always see adults playing *in school*. And they must. It's a case of leading by example. If teachers and supervisors join in with games – *really* join in, with all the running and silliness that involves – children love it. Games are suddenly Great Fun, and they want to play them over and over again. I think sometimes teachers are reluctant to join in because they are worried they will lose respect. Let's face it, there is nothing dignified about lying down on the ground, pretending to be a dead man; there is nothing elegant about hitching up your skirt and running round a circle in *Blade*! But it *does* show the children that you're a good sport, you're fun to be with, and you don't take yourself too seriously.

If I am leading a workshop in a school, and I see the teacher has put on her trainers, I know it'll be a good session. A teacher who plays alongside her class develops an easy rapport with them that is a joy to behold. Children willingly share their thoughts and ideas with her, because she's like a friend. And there's no loss of respect; these teachers are positively *adored*.

Last year, I did twelve sessions in an infant school, and afterwards, the headteacher asked me which class I had most enjoyed being with, and which class I had liked least. The class I liked best was Class X. The young teacher was great fun, and had enthusiastically played every game. The worst class was Class Y. The children were inattentive, disobedient and played the games almost reluctantly. Their teacher had sat at the side of the hall marking books for the first half of the session, and had disappeared for the second. The head nodded and smiled knowingly. 'Just as I would expect,' she said.

Q The children won't hold hands, so they are missing out on some really good games. Can this be overcome?

When does a child become too old to hold hands? It's an interesting question! Curiously, the answer seems to depend on the school. In tiny village schools, where children of all ages have to play together to make up numbers, they will happily hold hands right up to the age of eleven. In most schools, however, noses are definitely wrinkling by nine, and maybe even at *seven* if they have been told by older children that holding hands is for babies. This is a great shame, because nothing quite beats the exhilaration of chasing as a pair, holding hands. Two can't actually run as fast as one, but it doesn't *feel* like that! And running with a partner requires co-operation and consideration. These are skills worth exercising in the playground.

Many of the games I teach to Year 6 children involve holding hands – *Arch Tig* (see page 27), *Twister* (see page 29), *Lift Off!* (see page 37), *Quicksand* (see page 37) and *The Muscle Machine* (see page 45) – but they never complain! There are three reasons for this. First, these are clearly grown-up games. They are challenging and physical, not of the holding-hands-and-skipping-round-in-a-circle variety. Games *must* be suitable for the age of the class. Secondly, in these games holding hands serves a practical purpose: it's all about balance, and if you don't hold hands *you will fall over*. And thirdly, I am careful with my language, instructing them to *join* rather than *hold* hands.

There is an alternative way of joining hands. It's a grip, rather than a hold. You curl your fingers over, your friend does the same, and you join by interlocking the curls. This is a firm hold, but it's easy to release and can be used in chasing games like *Arch Tig* and *Touch and Go* (see page 27).

For circle games like *Dead Man Arise!* (see page 25) – which eleven-year-olds love, except for having to hold hands – children can hold wrists. This is not a safe hold for a chasing game, or for physical games like *Twister* and *Quicksand*. For these you must insist on *proper* hand-holding. There is no alternative!

Q One boy in my class won't join in, no matter how much I encourage him. What can I do?

First of all, you have to consider whether there's a medical condition behind this behaviour. For years, hundreds of 'odd' children have struggled through school – strangely withdrawn, prone to interrupting mid-sentence, unable to make friends – and now we learn they were actually suffering from Asperger's Syndrome. Mild autism can cause problems in the playground. Some autistic children, for example, are unwilling to hold hands. I remember one boy who wouldn't wear the coloured band I gave him simply because it was red, and he *never* touched red.

If there is an underlying medical condition, of course, it will show itself in the classroom as well as in the playground. If this behaviour *only* happens in the playground, the cause can be obscure, and children are frequently unwilling to discuss it. If they avoid running games, there might be a physical problem that worries them: they start to feel sick, or one knee feels funny. Perhaps they avoid them because they have been teased in the past about how they *look* when they run. Children can be super-sensitive to comments, and one cruel remark can put them off certain games for life. Even well-intentioned advice can cause problems. In one of my sessions there was an overweight girl who disliked running, and her father, hearing about the workshop, had told her to watch. This was reasonable enough advice for strenuous chasing games, but the girl was following it rigidly, sitting out of *every* game, even static ones like *Sausages* (see page 43). In another school, one girl refused to hold hands because her parents had told her that hands were 'dirty things'.

Being rejected causes concern for many children. Because it has happened to them before, they reckon it'll happen again – and they're right! It will! Children can be incredibly cruel when a game requires a specific number of players. One child will just be dropped, with a curt: '*We're* playing *this* now' by way of explanation. To make matters worse, it's usually done without any discussion. It's a unanimous decision, and invariably the same child is rejected every time. Being unwanted whenever teams are picked is also a soul-destroying experience.

It's no wonder that vulnerable children prefer to sit on the sidelines. It's the only way they can protect themselves from ritual humiliation. The trouble is, games change so quickly. One minute they can be enjoying a game of tig, and then suddenly, someone's suggested *Twister* and they're dropped! Better to sit out right from the start.

Using a questionnaire is a good way of discovering hidden playground worries. It can be slipped into an English lesson under the pretext of learning how to fill in forms. As well as asking the children what they like/dislike about playtime and playing games, it can ask them to suggest improvements.

Finally, there are some children that simply don't like games! It's not a problem for them, they just don't enjoy playing. Perhaps they would rather read. If there is a specially designated quiet area, with benches and some shelter from the wind, it provides these children with a positive reason for not joining in. They have chosen to read rather than play, and no further explanation should be necessary. Other children might prefer to be 'on duty' at playtime – as litter monitors, perhaps. Some might even welcome the chance to be games leaders, strange as that sounds! Perhaps they enjoy playing games, but fare badly with their peers, and would be far happier encouraging infants to play. It's a thought…

Q Is it worth buying play equipment?

I don't like to use too much equipment. I occasionally use a beanbag or a blanket, and I think chalk is wonderful: designing pitches encourages children to think visually. But when children have equipment, they start to rely on it. Take it away, and they can't think of anything to do. They can be very lazy with equipment too, and the novelty soon wears thin. Girls will wander around, holding hula hoops around their middles like crinolines, but not actually using them. It's *their turn* to have them, though, and they're going to make darn sure that that no one else gets near!

This is the main problem with small equipment. Hoops, balls, beanbags, skipping ropes, skittles and stilts: there can never be enough to go around! Strict rotas have to be introduced so everyone has a turn, but this kills spontaneity, and there will still be fights. Children will lose interest in something, walk away, and then return to find *someone else has picked it up*. They will steal a beanbag from someone and throw it up on the roof, rather than give it back. They will use skipping ropes as horses' reins, whips and for tying people to trees. Bats make good weapons. Soft balls are useless (but ripping them apart is good fun). Stilts need constant adult supervision.

I am terribly biased, of course! There are schools where equipment is treasured and well used. Games monitors enjoy the responsibility of checking equipment at the end of every break. Lunchtime supervisors share their skipping skills, and parents raise funds to renew worn items. It all works wonderfully well.

I am more enthusiastic about large play equipment, like climbing frames. I especially like pieces which encourage fantasy play, like wooden dragons or huge toadstools. Boats and trains are even better, because they suggest journeys. It's great to see half a dozen children clamber into a cement boat and sail off on an imaginary adventure. Tents can be exciting too. I know several schools that hire large ones for the summer term. A tent provides shade when it's hot, shelter when it rains – and it makes a wonderful outdoor classroom.

Q How can I stop children pulling each other's clothes/hogging being on/deliberately cheating?

It would be so easy if children played this way because they didn't know any better. Unfortunately they *do* know better. They understand the concept of fairness, and will quickly challenge unfair behaviour – when it's working against them. They know what is acceptable behaviour and what is not; they know the rules. They simply choose to play beyond the boundaries.

Only infants have the excuse of not understanding, and even they will be quick to learn. For a little one, it's a real achievement to deliberately catch hold of someone in a chasing game, however they do it! Learning how to tig can be learned later (see 'Games for infants', page 12) along with 'how to play nicely'.

But juniors and older infants really do know how to play nicely. When asked to define it, they repeat it like a mantra: no kicking, no pulling, no pushing, no pinching, no grabbing, no cheating. They have heard it so often, it has ceased to have any real meaning.

Not everyone cheats, of course, and the kickers and punchers are thankfully a minority, but many children play against the spirit of the game. By this, I mean that they manipulate the action, to benefit either their friends or themselves. Into this category comes hogging being on; deliberately trying to get caught; favouring friends all the time; freezing out the other sex (boys chasing only boys and vice versa); peeping when eyes should be closed and blurting out secrets in a guessing game. Very often, the culprits don't see these things as cheating. They don't do it to spoil their friends' fun (unless they are being malicious for the sake of it); rather they do it to enhance their own enjoyment, and they generally believe that no one notices them doing it. How wrong they are.

This is the starting point for an extremely effective talk I give to children called 'Why you should play fair'. I include it here verbatim, rather than discussing its content. With a little tinkering, you will be able to make it work equally well for your juniors. Again, it is designed to appeal to their self-interest.

WHY YOU SHOULD PLAY FAIR

For *years* now you have been told: you must play fair. Over and over: you must play fair. And you *know* what that means. You know how to play fair.

But I'm sure, by now, there are days when you think: why? Why should I play fair? Because I bet you all know someone who doesn't play fair, and who seems to get away with it. Someone who seems to bend the rules and have more fun than you. And you look at them, and you think: hang on! I'm playing fair, and I'm getting this much fun (demonstrate a small portion with your hands) but he's cheating and he's getting this much fun (demonstrate a large portion). I think I'll be a bit more like him!

Well – no. It doesn't work like that. And so, if you have ever wondered *why* you should play fair, I'll tell you. It's because *you are being watched*. It doesn't matter where you are – whether you're behind a tree, or behind the sheds – whenever you are out in the playground, you are being watched. And do you know who is watching you? It's your friends. They see everything you do. And if they don't like something, they'll remember it, and one day they'll use it against you.

You might get away with it for a week… a month… a term… maybe even a year or more if you're really good fun, but one day, they will just decide they've had enough. And they'll say: I'm not going to play with Jonathan any more. He's so *rough*. And I'm not going to play with Gopal; he grabs hold of my jumper all the time, instead of tigging properly. And I'm not going to play with Sophie, because she's so *bossy*; she tells everyone what to do. And Frank –

well, Frank just *argues* with you whenever he's out, and when he doesn't get his own way he just *sulks*. And I'm not going to play with Billie, because she picks her best friend all the time. And Daniel *cheats*. He thinks we don't notice, but we do! He cheats all the time, and it's *not fair*!

And on that terrible day, when your friends decide they don't want to be with you any more, they'll just desert you. And off they'll go, and you'll be all alone, sitting on a bench with just a packet of crisps for company. That will be a very sad day, and I would hate to see it happen to any of you. But it doesn't have to happen. It's up to you. Don't turn yourself into the Playground Pain! Play nicely, and people will *want* to be with you.

They'll say: where's Jenny? I really like Jenny: she's such good fun. And where's Kyle? He knows *loads* of games, and he always makes sure I have a go being on. And Phoebe is great. The other day, I fell over, and she took me to the staffroom and made sure I was all right. She's lovely. And Sam just *laughs*! Even when he's out, he laughs and gets on with it. And they'll come looking for you, and you'll never be short of friends.

And so *that* is why you should play fair. It's because it's *in your best interests* to do so. If you're rough; if you cheat; if you rip people's clothes; if you want your own way all the time; if you bully people – they won't *like* you. And we all want to be liked, don't we? And we all need friends. They are very precious things, and when you move on to the *big* school, you're going to need them. So look after them, and they will look after you.

It's up to you whether you fit names to real culprits. I never know the children I'm talking to, so I just pick names at random, but it's amazing how often I'm on target! There are howls of recognition, squeals of delight, fingers pointed and all kinds of denials made every time I use this speech. It gives children a chance to speak out for once, to say: 'You *do* do that! She's right!' Personalisation is the key, and although the tone is light-hearted, it does send out a very clear message. Try it!

GAMES MENU

GAMES MENU

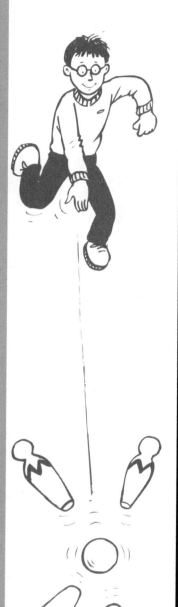

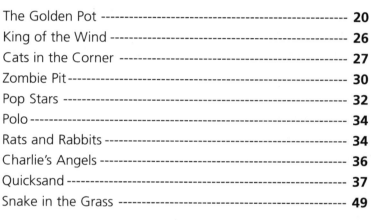

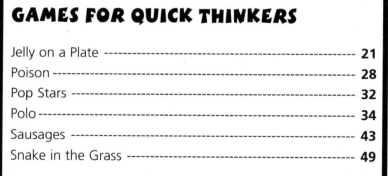